Michael Johnson Jr.

I'm ill Michael Jordan #23 The king of B-ball

OTHER BOOKS BY JEFF KINNEY

Diary of a Wimpy Kid

Diary of a Wimpy Kid: Rodrick Rules

Diary of a Wimpy Kid: The Last Straw

Diary of a Wimpy Kid: Dog Days

Diary of a Wimpy Kid Do-It-Yourself Book

Next in the series:

Diary of a Wimpy Kid 5

THE Wimpy Kid MOVIE DIARY

HOW GREG HEFFLEY WENT HOLLYWOOD

by Jeff Kinney

AMULET BOOKS

New York

Library of Congress Cataloging-in-Publication Data

Kinney, Jeff.
The wimpy kid movie diary / by Jeff Kinney.
p. cm.
ISBN 978-0-8109-9616-8
1. Diary of a wimpy kid (Motion picture) I. Title.
PN1997.2.W546K56 2010
791.43'72—dc22
2010001859

Book and cover design by Jeff Kinney

Published in 2010 by Amulet Books, an imprint of ABRAMS.

Printed and bound in U.S.A.
10 9 8 7 6 5 4 3 2 1

Amulet Books are available at special discounts when purchased in quantity for premiums and promotions as well as fundraising or educational use. Special editions can also be created to specification. For details, contact specialmarkets@abramsbooks.com or the address below.

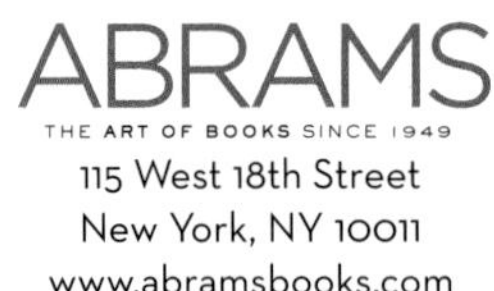

115 West 18th Street
New York, NY 10011
www.abramsbooks.com

TO ZACH AND ROBERT

A WIMP IS BORN

Greg Heffley was created in January 1998 in a small apartment in Massachusetts. There wasn't much to him, really. He was just a little pencil doodle in a cheap sketch pad.

One month later, Zachary Gordon was born on the other side of the country, in California. At that moment, Greg and Zach didn't really have a whole lot in common.

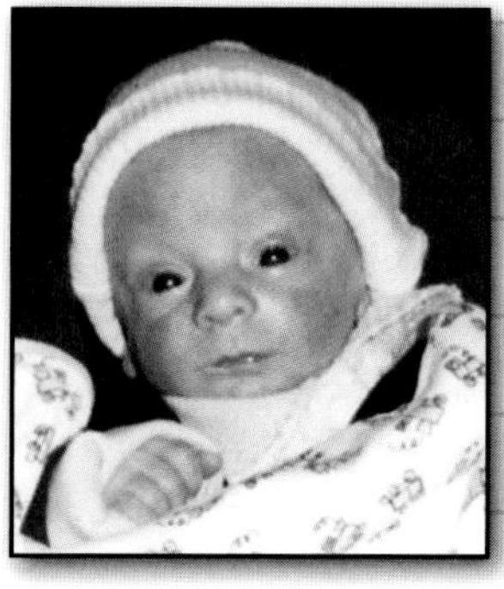

But eleven years later, the two would come together when Zach was chosen to play the part of Greg in the live-action "Diary of a Wimpy Kid" movie.

This book is the story of how a little idea got turned into a major motion picture, and how a fictional cartoon character became a real boy.

A ROUGH START

Greg Heffley didn't spring to life fully formed. Like any kid, Greg had to change and grow before he was ready to go out into the world on his own.

In fact, it took a really long time for Greg to develop into the character that he is today. Which is kind of strange, considering he's basically a stick figure.

HEY!

As you can see, Greg started off a little rough, but he evolved over time.

While Greg was going through major changes in the looks department, his stories were coming together. All the ideas for the "Diary of a Wimpy Kid" series were written down in the same sketch pad where Greg first appeared.

Each of the pages at the beginning of the sketch pad took a few hours to fill out.

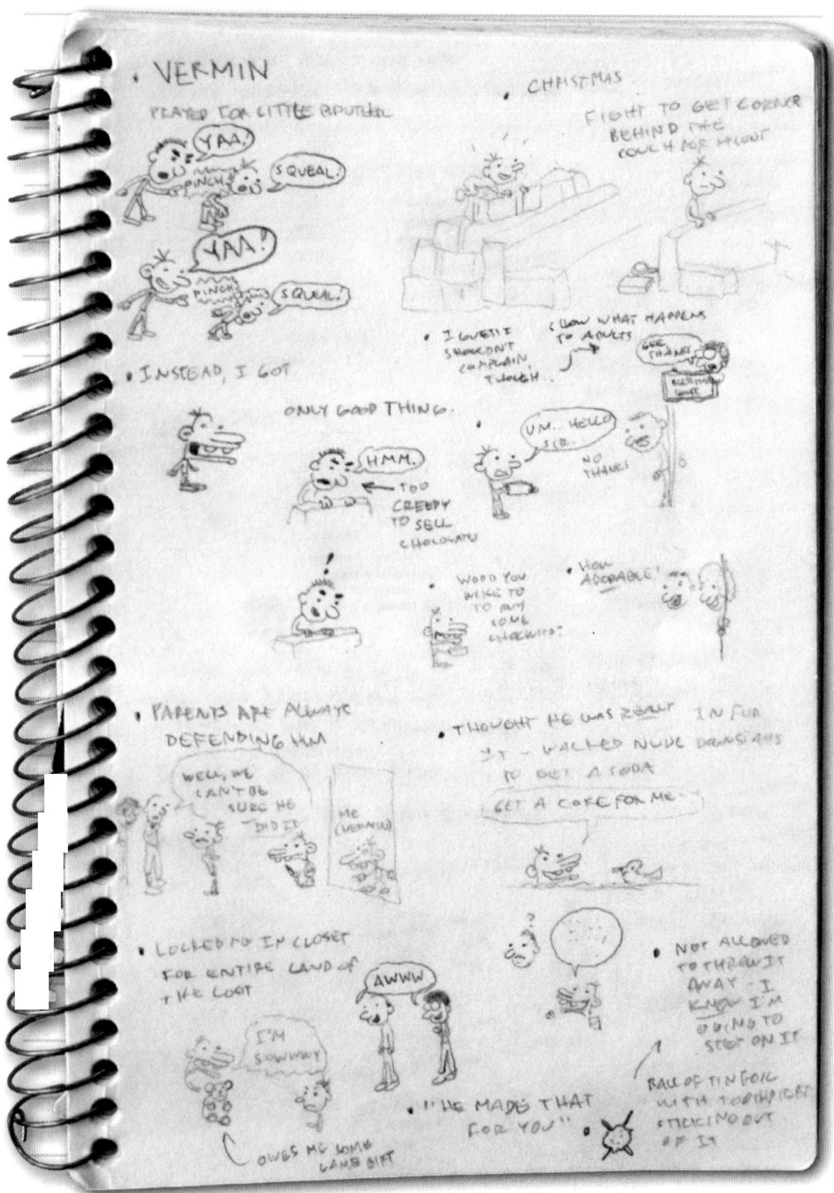

Over time, more and more ideas were crammed onto each page. The last few took several MONTHS to complete.

It took four years to fill up the sketch pad and create all the scenes and characters in the "Diary of a Wimpy Kid" universe. Right about the time the last idea was written down, Zach Gordon was celebrating his fourth birthday.

The pages of the sketch pad were photocopied, and each joke was cut out and stuck onto giant sheets of poster board. It took a few MORE years to put all the little pieces of paper in order and type them up in a single story.

The end result was a giant 1,300-page book that was first published online. More than 90% of the material written in the sketch pad didn't make the final cut.

A year later, an editor in New York decided to publish "Diary of a Wimpy Kid." And that's how Greg Heffley made the leap from a sketch pad to a printed book.

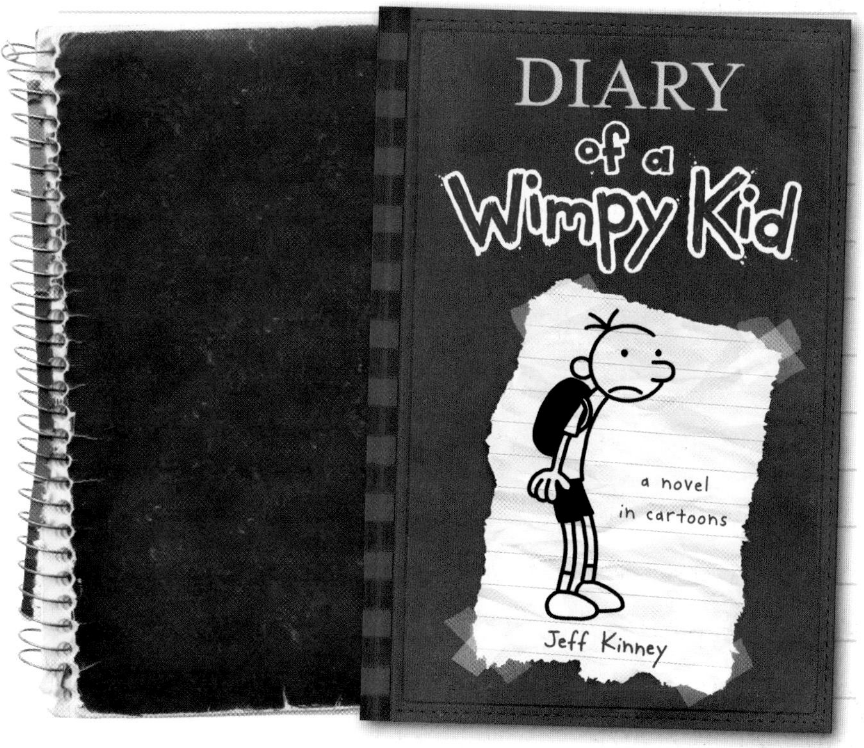

A few months later, Zach Gordon, now working as an actor in television and film, read the book and told his mom he hoped someone would make it into a movie. And if they did, he told her, he wanted to play the part of Greg Heffley.

MAKING IT REAL

Zach wasn't the only one thinking about making "Diary of a Wimpy Kid" into a movie. It turns out a few people in Hollywood were thinking the same thing.

But everyone had a different idea of what the film version should be.

A lot of people wanted to make big changes to the story and the characters. But finally, one movie studio came up with an idea that worked.

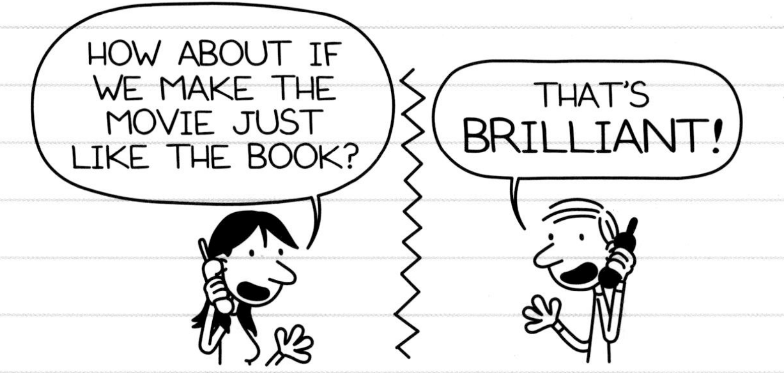

The idea of a live-action version of "Diary of a Wimpy Kid" raised some questions. How would fans of the book feel about Greg being played by a real actor? And would he look the way they thought he should? But there were even more important things to consider before moving forward.

GOING HOLLYWOOD

The studio executives and producers are the people responsible for getting the movie made. One of the first things they do is bring in writers to pitch their ideas for what should happen in the movie.

THE MOVIE OPENS WITH A CRANE SHOT OF A MIDDLE SCHOOL PLAYGROUND. A COLD WIND BLOWS ACROSS THE BASKETBALL COURT, SCATTERING LEAVES. THE CAMERA COMES TO REST ON A MOLDY PIECE OF CHEESE...

Once the studio and producers hear a pitch they like, they hire the writers to start working on the screenplay. A screenplay describes everything that happens in the film, from the action to the dialogue.

Here's how the opening scene of the "Diary of a Wimpy Kid" movie looks in the script—

INT. GREG'S BEDROOM 1
BLACK SCREEN. Soft breathing.

SUPER: "SEPTEMBER" is scrawled across the screen in Greg's handwriting.

Then BLINDING LIGHT.

RODRICK (O.S.)
Greg.

GREG'S POV: we find RODRICK HEFFLEY, an insolent sixteen-year-old, in our face. Rodrick is dressed for school.

RODRICK (CONT'D)
Greg!

GREG
(half asleep)
What?

Rodrick shakes GREG HEFFLEY, 12, awake in his twin bed.

RODRICK
What are you doing? Get up! Mom and dad have been calling you for an hour. You're gonna be late for your first day of middle school.

GREG
What?

Greg looks over at his clock. It reads 8:01AM

The writers try to include the most important stuff from the book, but they make changes, too. Some scenes and characters from the book are cut, and new ones are added. Sometimes the writers add new jokes and scenes to surprise the audience. Because let's face it—if everything that happens in the book happens in the film, there wouldn't really be a point in going to see the movie.

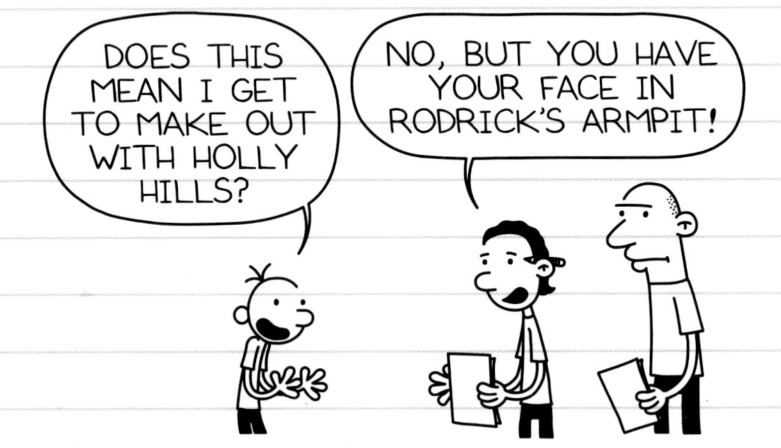

The screenplay goes through lots and lots of changes as the studio and producers make suggestions. Each time the writers turn in a screenplay, it's called a new draft. "Diary of a Wimpy Kid" went through about ten different drafts before filming began.

Not every idea makes it to the final draft. Here's part of a scene that was in the script early on but ended up getting cut—

RODRICK
Hey twerp, Dad brought home an ice cream cake so if you want some you better get your butt down there.

GREG
I don't know, I'm kind of in trouble.

RODRICK
Yeah, that's why they got it. Mom and dad feel bad about punishing you so hard.

Greg jumps up and rushes out the door.

INT. HEFFLEY HALLWAY - JUST LATER

Greg races down the stairs and skids to a stop in front of the open archway to the living room.

INT. HEFFLEY LIVING ROOM - CONTINUOUS

We see the Heffleys are having a quiet cocktail party with a few OTHER COUPLES. Everyone's dressed nicely, there is cheese and crackers, etc. on the coffee table. The adults all stare at Greg in his underwear, who awkwardly covers himself.

LOOKING FOR DIRECTION

While the studio and the producers were working with the writers on the screenplay, they were also busy looking for a director. After a long search, they chose Thor Freudenthal.

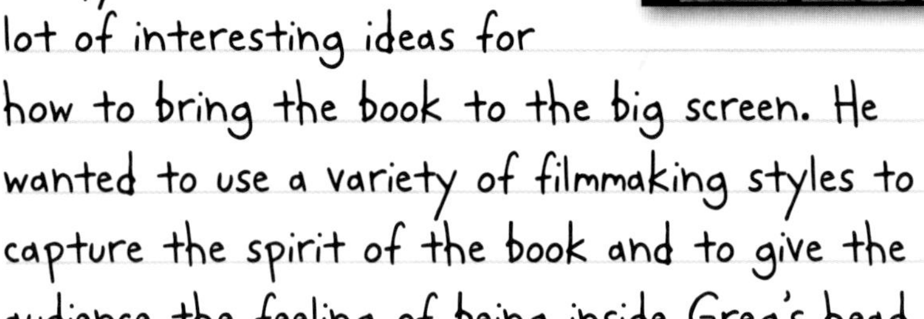

Thor (pronounced "Tor") was picked to direct "Diary of a Wimpy Kid" because he had a lot of interesting ideas for how to bring the book to the big screen. He wanted to use a variety of filmmaking styles to capture the spirit of the book and to give the audience the feeling of being inside Greg's head.

Before he became a director, Thor worked as a special effects artist and animator. Those skills would be very helpful in bringing the world of Greg Heffley to life. But there was something else that helped convince the producers Thor was the right person to direct "Diary of a Wimpy Kid."

As a boy, Thor kept a journal with illustrations, just like Greg. And if you're wondering why his entries aren't in English, it's because Thor grew up in Germany.

THE SEARCH FOR GREG

Once a director was chosen, the search was on for the kid who would play Greg Heffley.

It wasn't easy to find a kid who could fill Greg's cartoon shoes. You might've noticed that in the books, Greg isn't always such a likable character.

The kid chosen to play Greg would have to pull off a tough trick. He'd have to act like a bit of a jerk at times, but get the audience to root for him anyway.

Dozens of television and movie actors were brought in to try out for the part. They were asked to memorize Greg's opening monologue and recite it in front of the camera.

FIRST OF ALL, LET ME GET SOMETHING STRAIGHT...
DIARY

But no one seemed like a perfect fit. The studio and producers decided to do a nationwide search for Greg. They wrote up a description of the type of kid they were looking for and sent it out everywhere.

The character of Greg Heffley is slight, physically unprepossessing, and not overly cute or precocious. He has a quirky, memorable face, is bright and articulate, and possesses a vivid fantasy life—but he is cursed by the fact that he's in middle school. Auditioning actors must be able to handle dialog and have a flair for ironic comedy.

A website was even created to help with the search. Thousands of kids of all shapes and sizes showed up at casting calls and posted their auditions online.

In the end, Zachary Gordon got the part. Zach nailed his audition and left no doubt that he could bring the character of Greg Heffley to life. And who knows? Maybe this drawing, which Zach sent to the producers a few days before his eleventh birthday, helped him get the job—

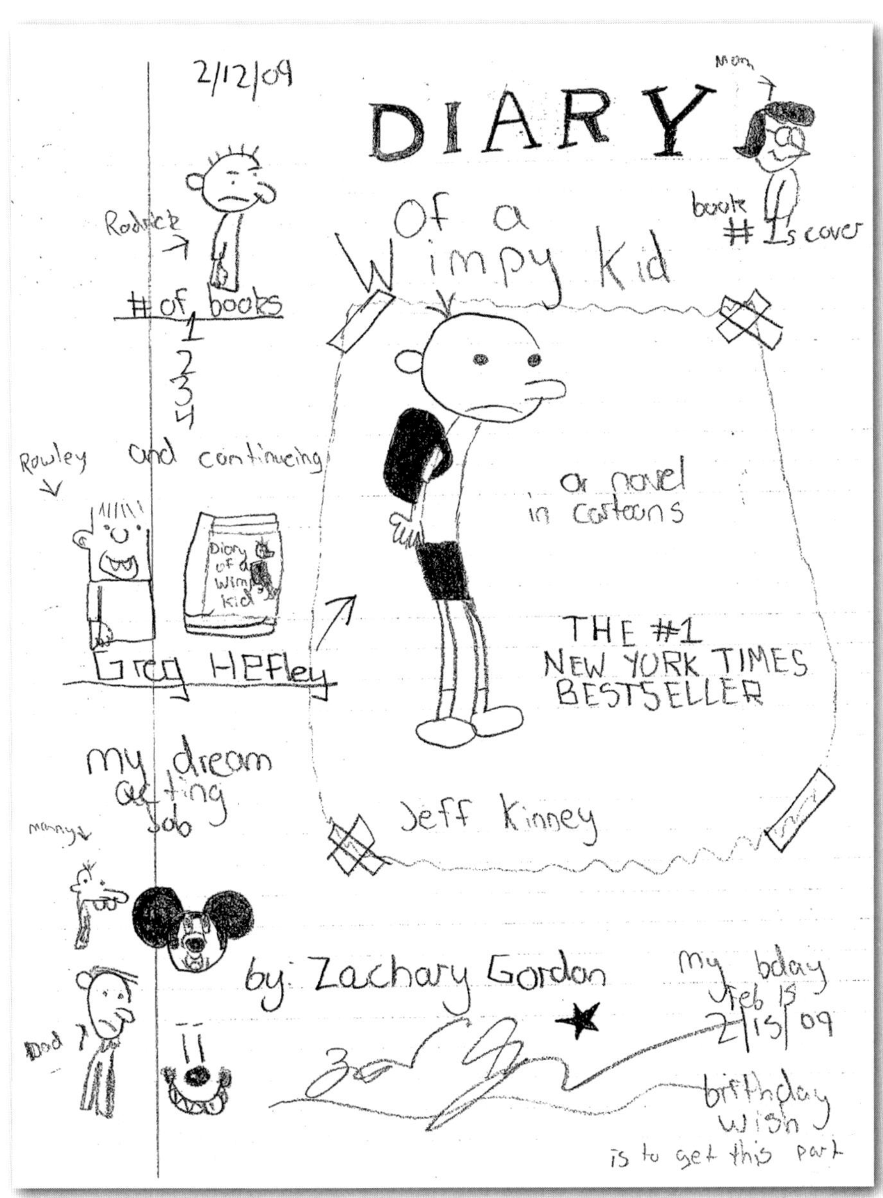

ZACH SAID HIS BIRTHDAY WISH WAS TO GET THE PART.

LOOKING FOR A FRIEND

What Greg needed next was a best friend. And of course Greg's best friend in the book is Rowley Jefferson.

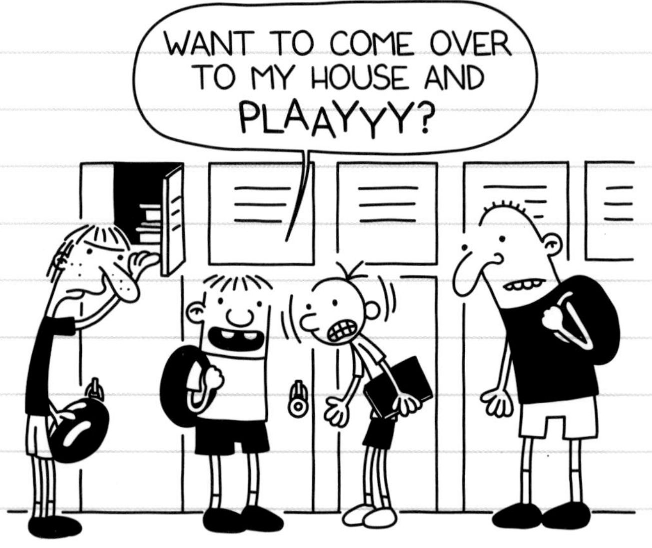

In many ways, Rowley is the opposite of Greg. Rowley is a happy, innocent kid and a loyal friend. Luckily, the perfect Rowley Jefferson was found in Rhode Island, and his name was Robert Capron. Robert had done some stage and film acting as well.

And like Zach, Robert drew a picture for the producers to show his enthusiasm for the part—

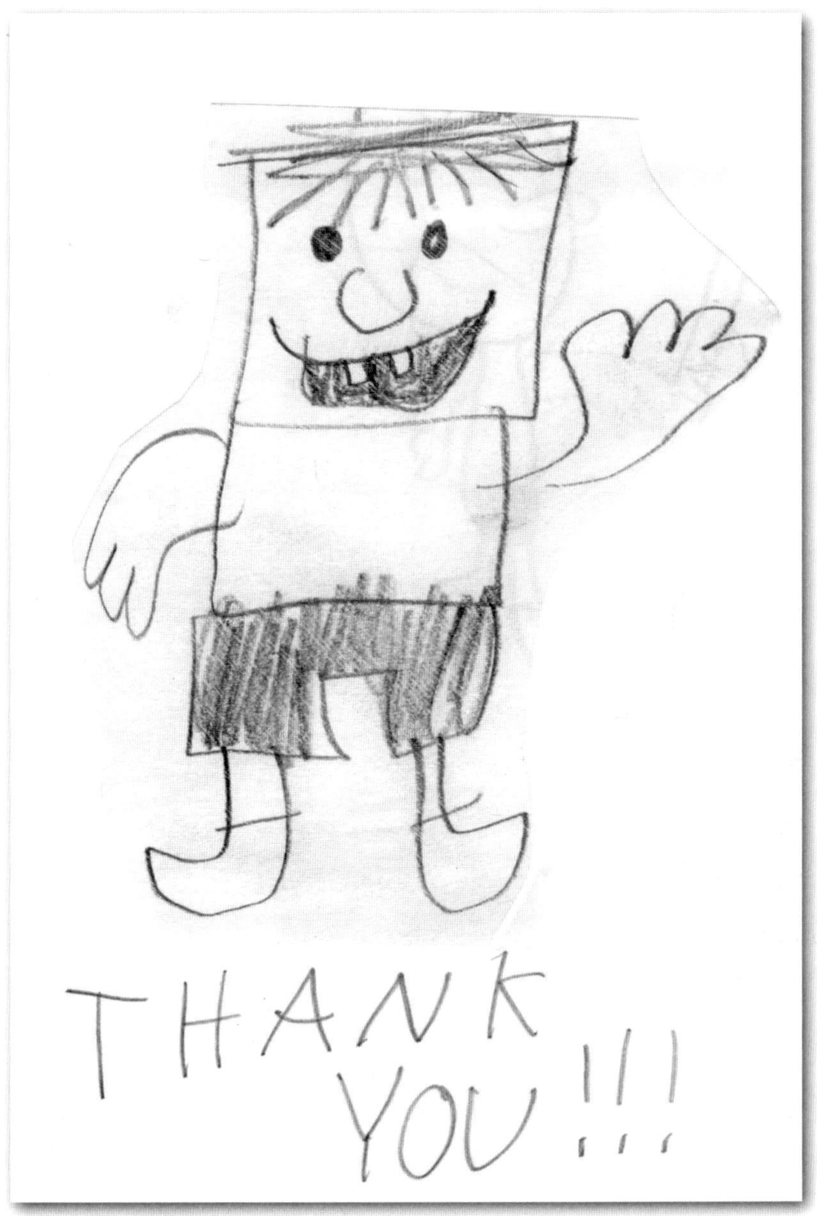

The next step was to get the two boys together and see if they had chemistry. In other words, were Zach and Robert believable as best friends? Robert was flown out to California, where he and Zach met for the first time.

The two boys did a screen test, which is a short scene that's filmed to see how the actors work together on camera. The actors performed in an empty environment with almost no props or background scenery.

For the screen test, Greg lectured Rowley about wearing clothes that are more "middle school friendly." This scene made it into the final movie, but it looked completely different.

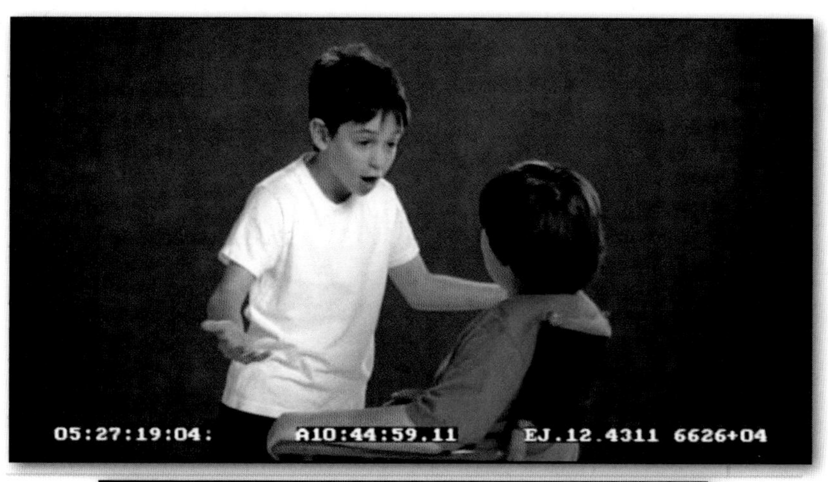

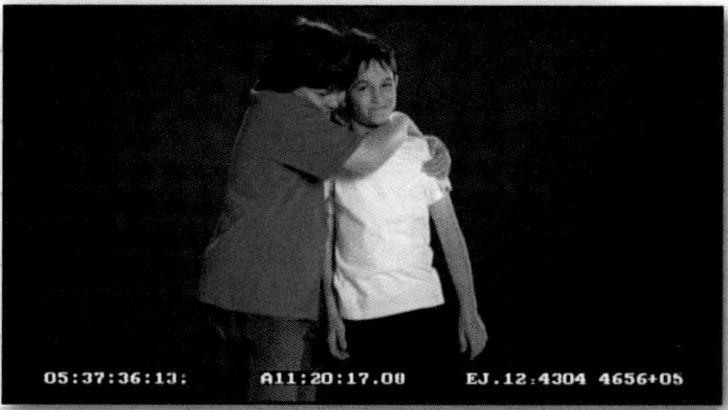

Everyone felt the boys had real chemistry and did a great job bringing Greg and Rowley and their complicated friendship to life.

HOMEWORK?

To help Zach and Robert get into their roles, Thor asked each boy to write an essay from his character's point of view. Zach typed his essay.

Diary of a Wimpy Kid

Greg Hefley's Perspective

In middle school I'm basically the only mature and normal student. For example my best friend Rowley is sort of a 4th grader because he acts like it, but I'll fix him up in no time, the good thing about him is he's warm hearted and doesn't really know how to act like a normal 6th grader but he is really lucky he has me.

My mom really doesn't get me all that well, I mean, she knows I'm in middle school but she treats me like a kid. And my dad, don't even get me started on my dad, the funny thing is he'd rather play with his miniature battlefield than hang out with his children or his family. WHICH IS FINE WITH GREG, UNTIL TRAGEDY NIGHT.

So yeh, my brother Rodrick is such a jerk he just finished giving me a prep-talk with his unshaved armpit hairs in my face. He always tortures me in ways no ordinary teenager could think of, it's like he's incredibly smart when it comes to torturing me, but he's not good in school, kind of funny, huh? HE WOULD NOT COME OUT WITH THE TRUTH

My little obnoxious baby brother Manny is like Rodrick the second, he always makes these weird grunting

Robert wrote his essay out by hand.

Hi! My name is Rowley Jefferson. I am just moving into middle school, and I love it! It's amazing I got this far in life already.

I was born in Ohio, and moved here around the age of 5. I've always loved my parents, even though they can be strict. My parents are very rich, so we go on vacations a lot. I love going to new places, especially Europe. That's when I first heard about Joshie. He's the best singer ever! And then there's when I went to Australia. G'day, mate! Anyway, I love having fun, especially with Greg. Greg's my best friend, and we play all the time.

He's a really nice guy, although sometimes we don't agree on things. Like going into his brother Rodrick's room, or acting like somebody else. But we're still great friends.

I don't think I like people that are mean. They're not very nice, and you can't have fun with them. And people that lie are difficult,

Zach and Robert both proved they understood their characters and were ready to get started.

THE PERFECT SPOT

Now that the two lead actors, or principals, were chosen, it was time to figure out where the movie would be filmed.

But here's the thing: In the "Wimpy Kid" books, there aren't really any clues about where the stories take place. No states or cities are mentioned. However, since the characters celebrate Halloween and Thanksgiving, you know they live in the United States. But you don't know if they live on the East Coast, the West Coast, or somewhere in the middle.

The reason there aren't any geographic clues in the books is because the reader is supposed to believe the stories could've happened anywhere—across the country or right down the street.

The producers searched for a place that looked like a typical American town. They considered Rhode Island, Michigan, and lots of other places in the United States. So it's weird that they ended up finding the perfect American town in Canada.

Vancouver was chosen as the location for "Diary of a Wimpy Kid" because the houses and schools in the suburbs look just like the ones in the United States. Plus, lots of other movies are filmed in Vancouver. In fact, so many movies are made there that some people call it "Hollywood North."

ASSEMBLING THE TEAM

Once the location was chosen, the producers hired a team of people, called a crew, to get the movie made. A crew is made up of camera operators, sound and lighting technicians, hair and makeup artists, costume designers—basically, anyone who's involved with the movie and isn't an actor.

And here's where you can really start to see the biggest difference between writing a book and making a film: It only takes one person to write a book, but it takes hundreds of people to make a typical movie.

An author could write a whole book on a cheap pad of paper, but it costs millions of dollars to make your average Hollywood film.

MINIMUM BOOK REQUIREMENTS

MINIMUM MOVIE REQUIREMENTS

So where's it all spent? On camera and lighting rentals, food and hotels, set and costume design, transportation, and the money that's paid to the actors and crew.

The bottom line is that it's not cheap to make a movie, even if there aren't any big explosions or computer-generated aliens involved.

GREEN MEANS "GO"

With all the pieces in place—screenplay, director, lead actors, location, and crew—the studio was ready to give the movie the green light. Before that moment, things move slowly. But after the green light, everything happens all at once.

Zach and Robert were both winding down their school year on opposite sides of the country when the call came.

In an instant, each boy's life was turned upside down. They packed their bags and headed for Vancouver, each with one parent.

It would be three months before Zach or Robert went home.

By this time, everyone in Greg's family but Manny had been cast.

DAD (STEVE ZAHN) RODRICK (DEVON BOSTICK)

GREG (ZACH GORDON) MOM (RACHAEL HARRIS)

The actors were invited to Vancouver, where they met one another for the first time.

The cast participated in a "table read," where they go through the script from start to finish. This gives the director, writers, producers, and studio a chance to hear the script spoken by the actors for the first time, which helps to improve the dialogue.

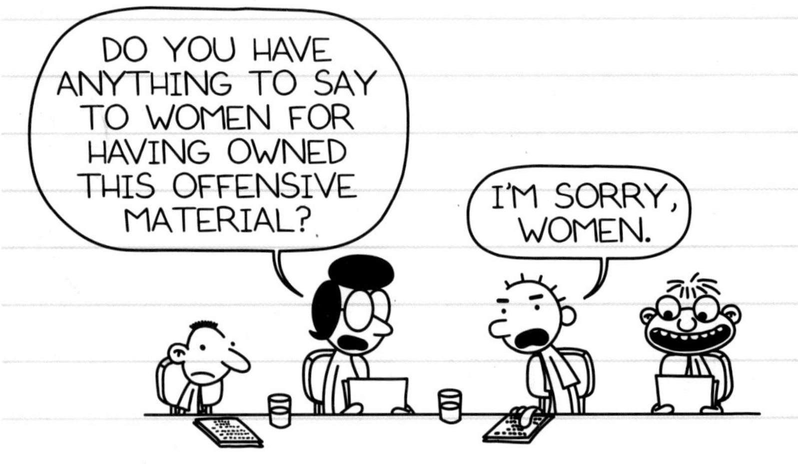

Working with people you've never met before and pretending they're your family members can be a strange experience. So the producers arranged for the newly minted Heffleys to have a few "family outings" to get to know each other. After the table read, Rachael Harris, Zach Gordon, and Devon Bostick had a bowling night.

A few weeks later, when Steve Zahn arrived on the scene, the group went out for their first-ever meal as a family.

FILLING OUT THE RANKS

Every role in the movie had to be filled, from Greg's arch-enemy, Patty Farrell, to the kid who starts the Cheese Touch, Darren Walsh.

PATTY FARRELL
(LAINE MACNEIL)

DARREN WALSH
(HARRISON HOUDE)

A casting director looked through thousands of résumés and photos before bringing in actors to audition. The producers then made a final decision for each part.

Since "Diary of a Wimpy Kid" was filmed in Vancouver, most of the kids you see in the movie are from the general area. But the roles of Fregley and Chirag were played by actors from the United States.

Grayson Russell (Fregley) is from Alabama, and Karan Brar (Chirag) lives in Washington state. Fregley and Chirag each have small parts in the book, but their roles were beefed up for the movie.

FREGLEY
(GRAYSON RUSSELL)

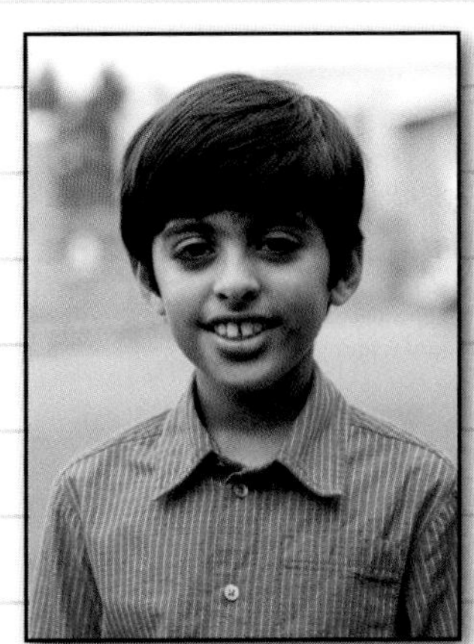

CHIRAG
(KARAN BRAR)

DOUBLE TROUBLE

One of the trickiest roles to cast was Greg's three-year-old little brother, Manny. You might have noticed that in the books, Manny looks sort of like a bucktoothed alligator. Unfortunately, there aren't many kids who look like that in Vancouver, or anywhere else for that matter.

SNIFF

So the casting director looked for the next best thing, which was a cute kid with a memorable face. After a lot of searching, the perfect Manny was found. Two of them, actually.

CONNOR AND OWEN FIELDING

The trouble with three-year-olds is that they don't always do exactly what you want them to do, so it's a good idea to have a backup in case one of them decides not to cooperate.

The other funny thing about three-year-old actors is that they're not actually aware they're actors. That means they're not too concerned with memorizing their lines or rehearsing. One second they're minding their own business, and the next they're making a movie.

GIRLS IN THE WIMPY WORLD

Another challenge was picking the girls who would play Greg's classmates. In the "Diary of a Wimpy Kid" books, most girls look very similar to one another. In fact, the only thing that sets them apart is their hair.

Boys, on the other hand, look very different from one another in the books.

So why is that? Well, remember, Greg's journal is told from his point of view, so we're seeing things through his eyes. And Greg thinks all girls are more or less the same, so that's why they're drawn the same.

That's because Greg doesn't really "get" girls yet. Girls are a mystery to him. He doesn't understand why they travel in packs and go to the restroom in pairs.

Of course, you can't cast a movie with a bunch of young actresses who all look exactly the same. So the girls in the "Diary of a Wimpy Kid" movie look very different from one another, like they do in real life.

ANGIE
(CHLOE MORETZ)

Just don't expect Greg to be able to tell them apart.

A CHEESY VILLAIN

Every movie needs a good villain, and this movie was no exception. The thing is, the villain in "Diary of a Wimpy Kid" isn't a person—it's a dairy product.

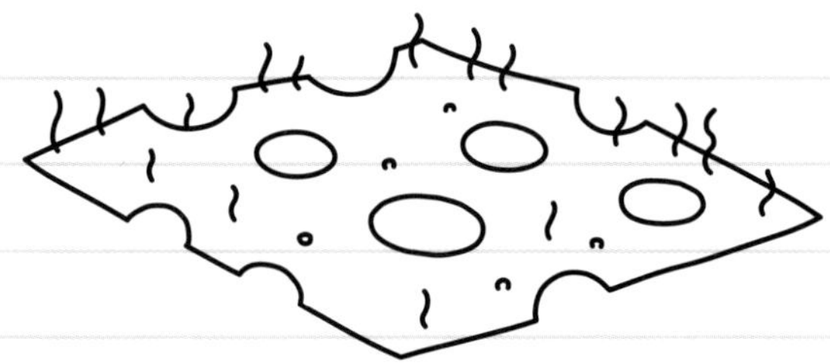

Yes, the villain in the movie is a piece of cheese. But finding the right piece of cheese was just as difficult as finding the actors for the other important roles.

SORRY, YOU'RE A LITTLE TOO TALL FOR THE PART.
I'VE GOTTA GET A NEW AGENT.

All different types of cheese were considered for the part—cheddar, American, provolone—but in the end, a large, deli-cut slice of Swiss cheese beat out the competitors.

To find out what would happen to cheese if it was left out in the sun, a real piece was placed on the ground, then covered with wire mesh to keep animals out and let the weather in. This allowed the cheese to "age" and gave the moviemakers a chance to study the effects of sun, rain, and cold air.

When the Cheese is shown up close in the movie, it's not really there at all—it's a computer graphic. The visual effects department used a piece of silicone as a starting point, then digitally added stages of decay.

STAGE ONE

The silicone "blank" for the Cheese. The digital aging effects were painted on this model.

STAGE TWO

The Cheese as it looked on the first day of school.

STAGE THREE

After a few months the Cheese gets a little moldier and nastier.

STAGE FOUR

The Cheese looks good enough to eat.

THE MASTER PLAN

A person called a "line producer" then took the finished script and started working on the shooting schedule. Every minute of every day has to be planned out in advance, because going into overtime is very expensive. The schedule is actually like a giant puzzle, and the scenes are the pieces.

The trick is to make all the pieces fit together so the movie can get made on time and under budget.

What makes the planning so tricky is that a movie isn't shot in order, from beginning to end. The reason for that is because it's more efficient to film all the scenes that take place in a certain location back-to-back so the crew doesn't have to keep moving the equipment from one place to another.

While the line producer was working out the schedule, the director was doing some planning of his own. Thor had begun creating storyboards for the movie to plan out each shot.

A storyboard is a series of panels that describes everything that goes on in a scene—which actors are in a shot, how they're moving, and where the camera is positioned. For most movies, an artist is hired to create storyboards, but for "Diary of a Wimpy Kid," Thor drew his own.

WITH GREG AS HE STEPS ONTO STREET.
GREG: "WE'RE CALLING THE COPS!"
TRUCK BRAKES

GETTING INTO CHARACTER

Once all the actors in the movie were cast, it was time to start creating costumes.

You might not think of the characters in "Diary of a Wimpy Kid" as wearing costumes, since most of the time they're dressed in everyday clothes. But a lot of thought and work actually went into each character's wardrobe.

The first thing the costume designers did was look to the book for inspiration. But that wasn't much help, since most of the characters wear the same thing all the time.

It would be kind of boring and a little unrealistic for the live-action Greg to be wearing a white shirt and black shorts every day. So a whole wardrobe was created to cover the school year.

Costumes are more than just clothes. They give you extra information about the characters. Greg's wardrobe is made up of outfits that are a little too tight, to emphasize his smallness in the world. And Greg's shirts and pants are a little worn-out because his older brother, Rodrick, had them first. So Greg feels frustrated that he never gets anything new.

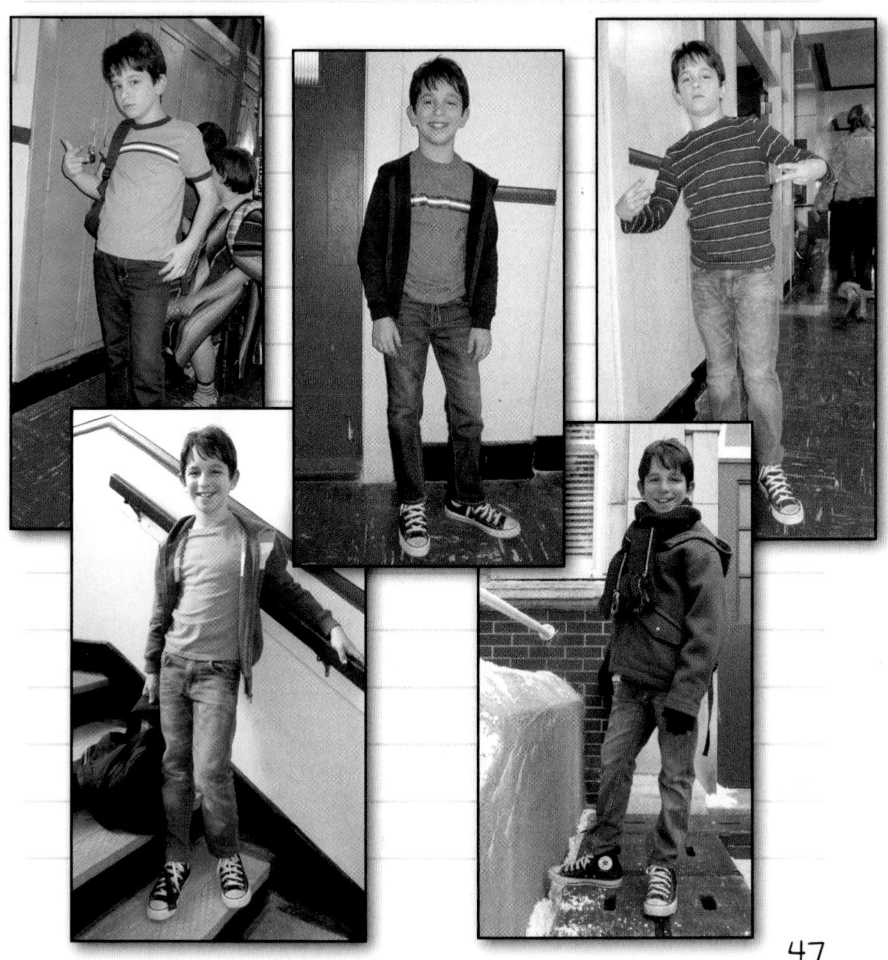

Manny, on the other hand, is always dressed in brand-new clothes. That tells you he gets special treatment from his parents.

Even Manny's Halloween outfit is a deluxe version of Greg's costume.

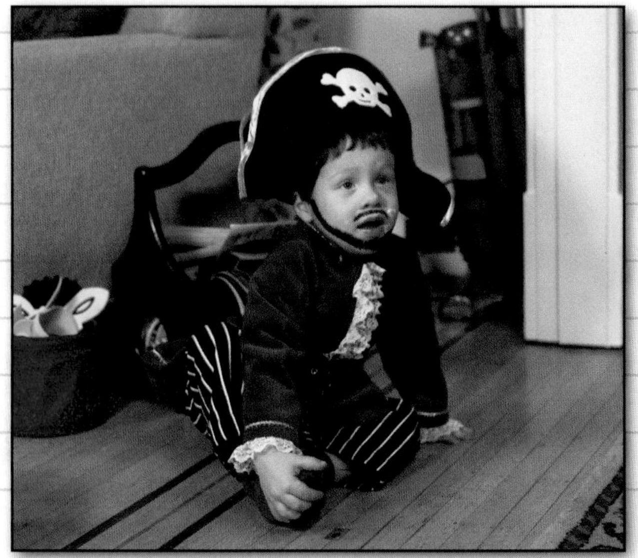

Rowley's outfits look comfortable but unstylish. His clothes are a mix of men's and husky sizes. They make him a nonconformist without his really knowing it.

Unlike Greg, Rowley isn't concerned with looking cool. His mom dresses him in clothes that make him feel safe and happy.

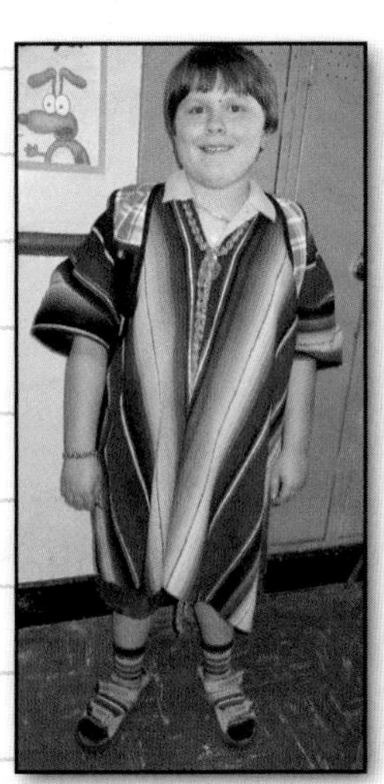

Sometimes Rowley wears clothes from foreign countries. Rowley has done a lot of traveling with his family, which gets on Greg's nerves because he's a little jealous of his friend.

Fregley is an oddball character, and he dresses completely different from his classmates.

Fregley's mom is a seamstress, and she makes all her son's clothes. She uses a lot of old fabrics, and you get the feeling that she might even be making some of his clothes out of pajama materials.

It's clear that Fregley's mom loves her child but doesn't have a clue as to what a normal middle school student might wear. Fregley's wardrobe also tells you he couldn't care less about fitting in with his peers.

One of the biggest challenges the costume designers faced was to make the outfits in the movie look timeless. While the story is meant to feel like it could've happened in any PLACE, it's also meant to feel as if it could have happened at any TIME.

So the costume designers bought and made clothes that felt like they could have been worn by kids twenty years ago, or could be worn twenty years from now.

And not only did they have to put together outfits that looked timeless, but they also had to have multiple versions of each outfit. That way, if Robert spilled hot chocolate on his snowman sweater, the wardrobe department had a spare ready to go.

THE PERFECT SCHOOL

Location scouts drove around the Vancouver area looking for the right school to use in the movie. And they found it—well, actually, they found three of them. It took three real schools to make one fictional school.

Shaughnessy Elementary School was used for its exterior and outdoor basketball court.

Van Tech Secondary School was used for its gym.

And Templeton Secondary School was used for its hallways, classrooms, and auditorium.

In the movie, all three schools are combined to feel like one place: Westmore Middle School.

Westmore Middle School had to be convincing, so graphic designers got to work bringing it to life. The artists started by creating school colors, a mascot, and a logo.

Once that was finished, they moved on to designing print materials, like the school paper.

WESTMORE WARBLER

VOL.MMXI THIRD EDITION

A GREAT DAY FOR WOMEN

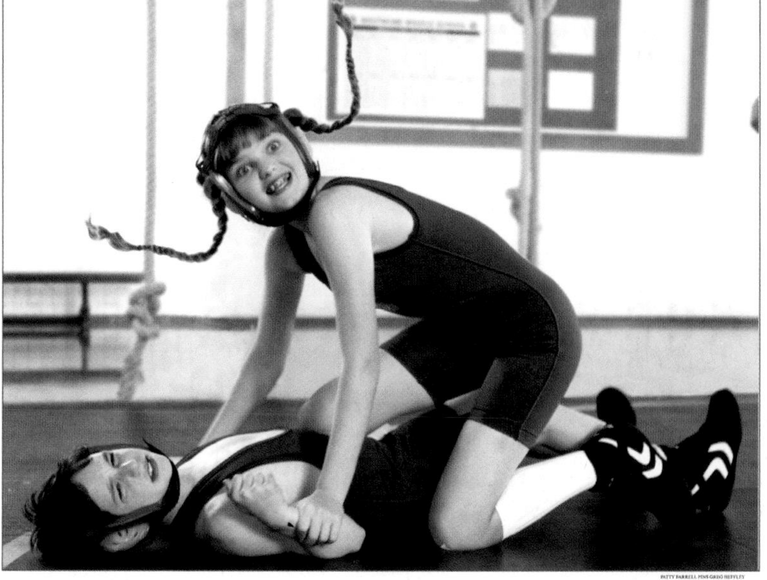

PATTY FARRELL PINS GREG HEFFLEY

The Westmore Middle School Hornets Wrestling team was more than proud to accept Patty Farrell into the ring, and in a suprising victory over Greg Heffley. The semi-final battle between Heffley and Farrell was again decided on the final match as Patty Farrell won a major decision. She was then named most outstanding wrestler in the finals. Patty Farrell pinned three opponents and won a 19-5 major decision over another to be named most outstanding wrestler. The Hornets travel to Hendersonville for the west regional of the individual state tournament on Friday. Best match of the night was at 115 lbs when 110 lb 3rd ranked Jonathon Taylor stepped up one weight class to take on Mike West (6th ranked at 115 lbs). The match was tied at 17-17 at the end of regulation time. Aguilar took just 33 seconds of the first overtime period to score and win 19-17 in his third title bout.

The "National Middle School Spirit of Sport Award" was created by the school to recognize those individuals who exemplify the ideals of the spirit of sport that represent the core mission of education-based athletics.

Green is one of the top wrestlers on the Hornets wrestling team, which comes as no surprise to the community. His father, who grew up in the same town, also was an outstanding wrestler for the school. Green's family was always there to support him, and rarely missed any of his matches.

On the way back from a tournament in February 2008, their vehicle was hit coming down a mountain by a semitrailer truck that had lost control. Green's parents and older brother Scott were in the vehicle at the time of the accident. Green's mother was killed on impact, and his father died several weeks later in the hospital. His brother was bed ridden for several months, but is learning to wrestle again after the accident.

The most competitive finals came at 155 pounds, when Madeleine Grant of Westmore scored a last-second reversal to defeat Deana Kittson, of Westmore 8-7. Grant was fifth in the Junior Nationals last summer.

In an all-Westmore final at 126 pounds, Steve Sach defeated Pete Whyte, 8-2. Sach was fifth at the Junior Nationals last year

Not suprising Saul West defeated Jeff Bonny in a match-up promting Bonny to stomp, and demand a re-match. During the re-match title fight West pinned Bonny in the first three minutes of the match. Bonny said in a post match interview "I never saw it coming, I knew he was strong but thought with my mental wit I could defeat him" We will be looking forward to future match up's with the two wrestlers.

Saul West's life coach John Dillard was pleased with outcome, and commented lightly on West's performance.

Printed on 100% recycled paper

The graphic designers even created a school yearbook. Here's the front cover—

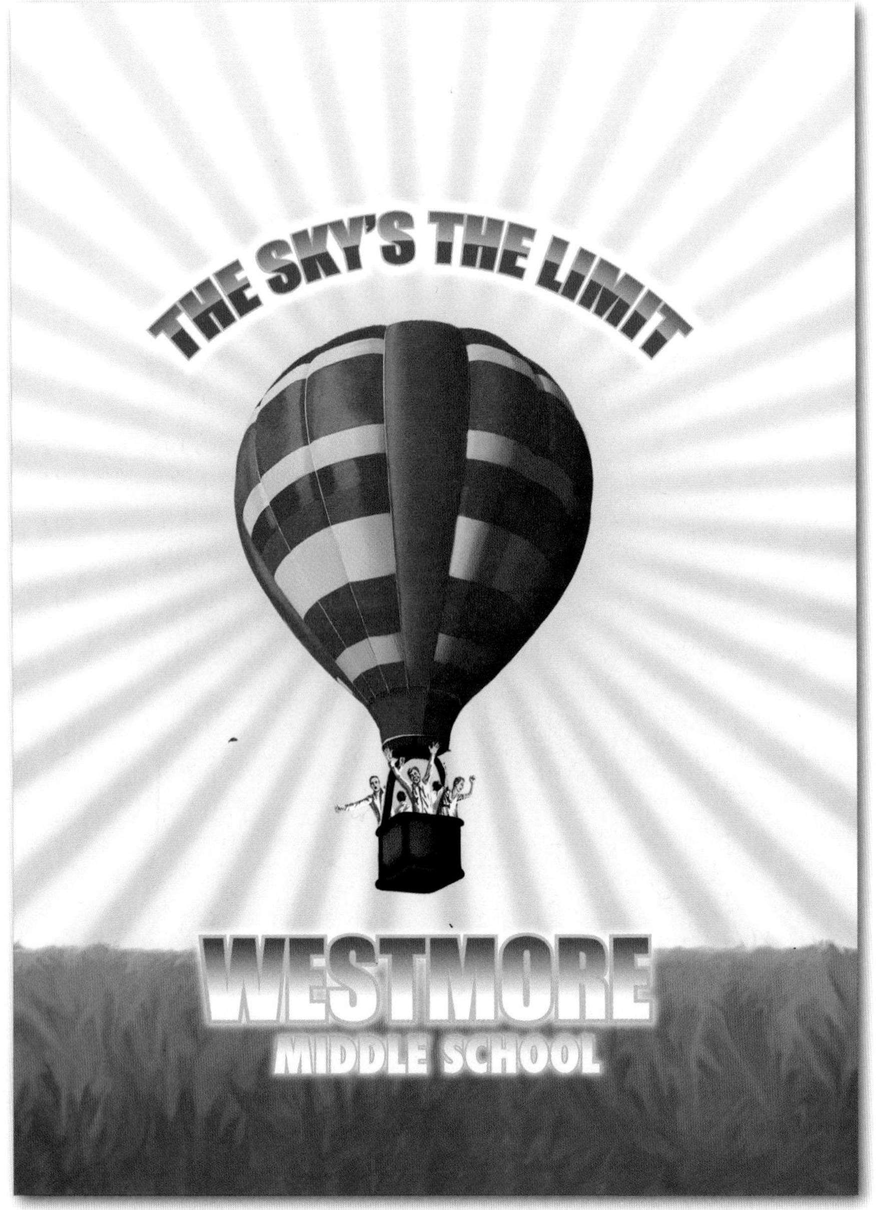

And here's one of the inside pages. Most of the kids in the photos were extras in the film—

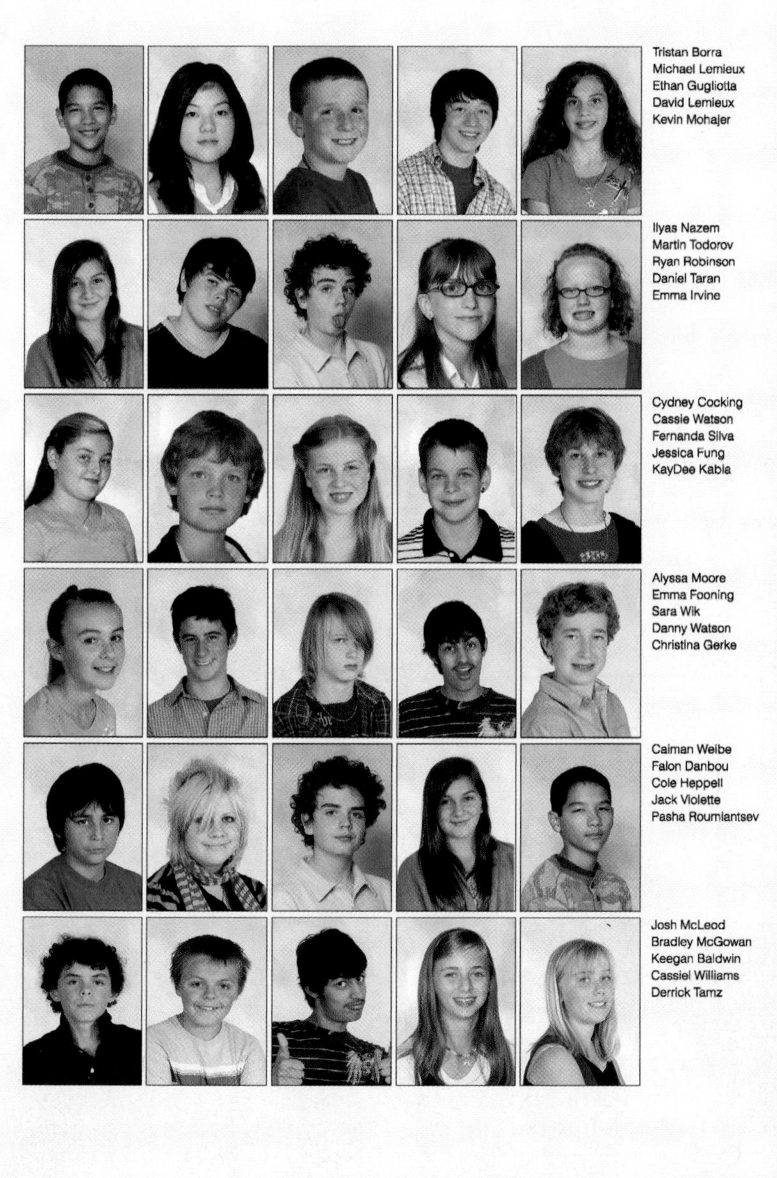

Next, set designers went into Templeton Secondary School to start transforming it into Westmore Middle School.

No detail was overlooked. Fake trophies were created to show off the accomplishments of Westmore's imaginary sports teams, and pictures of make-believe Westmore students were hung in the hallways.

If you look closely in the movie, you might even catch a picture of Preston Mudd, Athlete of the Month, hanging on one of the walls.

P. Mudd
Westmore Middle School
Athlete of the Month

The set designers repainted Templeton's hallways and classrooms with the Westmore school colors: blue and gold.

But if Westmore looked like it was freshly painted, it wouldn't be convincing. Westmore needed to feel broken in, so the painters used some tricks to age their work.

One of the techniques they used was to mix the color of the background that was being covered with the fresh paint, making it look faded. You can see the effect on this mural painted on a giant brick wall of Shaughnessy Elementary School.

Of course, no school would feel complete without posters and student-created artwork decorating the walls. Here are a few of the items that you'll see posted on bulletin boards and in the hallways—

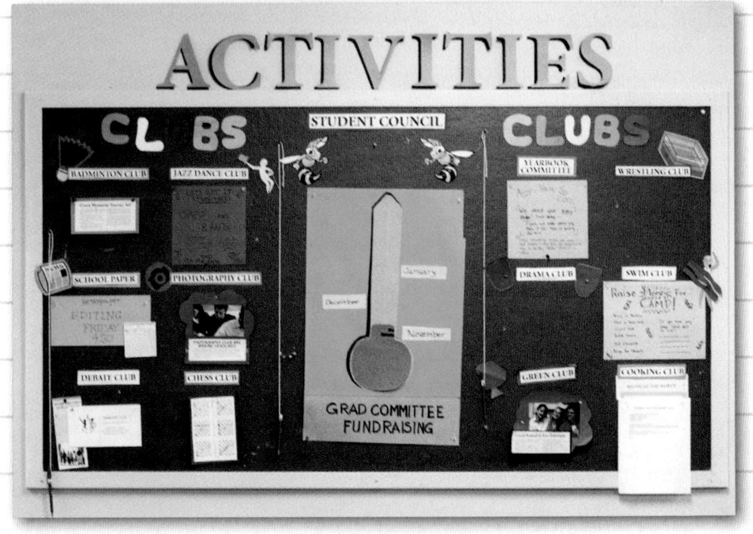

Here are some posters supposedly created by Bryan Little, the school cartoonist behind the "Wacky Dawg" comic strip—

The graphic artists made sure to use materials students could easily get their hands on, like poster board, colored pencils, and crayons.

You might remember that Greg Heffley entered an antismoking-poster contest in the book.

Be on the lookout for some of the other entries in the movie.

To create artwork that looked like it was made by middle schoolers, the graphic designers had to seriously suppress their talents.

There were lots of things created for the movie that are only on the screen for a split second. Here are some of Rowley's "Zoo-Wee Mama" comic strips.

If you blink when you're watching the movie, you might miss them.

Can't this hot air balloon go any higher?
Whatever you want, bub!
SSS
ZOO-WEE MAMA!
Hi, I'm from the future.
Did you come to tell me what the world of tomorrow will be like?
No, I came to witness the impact of meteor XLJ-42.
ZOO-WEE MAMA!
How does it feel to be the first person to make it to the end of this comic without saying "Zoo-Wee Mama"?
Um... Uh...
ZOO-WEE MAMA!
FAINT

One example of a set that was loaded with details was Mr. Winsky's office. Mr. Winsky is in charge of the safety patrols, and Greg and Rowley end up in his room a few times during the movie.

The art department created pictures and memorabilia for Mr. Winsky's office, to show how serious he is about safety.

It's clear from the stuff hanging on Mr. Winsky's walls that his glory days were when he was a safety patrol in middle school.

To give you an idea of how far the set designers and decorators will go to create a believable environment, they even created fake newspaper clippings showing Mr. Winsky as an adolescent. Real photos of the actor as a teen were used for the articles.

The art department wrote newspaper stories even though there's no chance the audience could read them during the movie.

Winsky Inducted Into The Safety Patrol Hall of Fame

Bertrand Winsky

Bertrand Winsky, a safety patrol captain and fifth-grader from Westmore Middle School was inducted into the Safety Patrol Hall of Fame. Winsky, is the son of Sgt. 1st Class Markand Winsky. He is one of 10 hall of fame winners across the state and was nominated for the award by Lori West, safety patrol advisor and paraeducator. "Winsky is a wonderful advocate and role model for Westmore students," said West. "He has boundless energy and a strong commitment to safety and community service. His organizational skills leadership and dedication make her very deserving of this honor." Winsky will be honored along with other hall of fame recipients at the May 1 baseball game. "I enjoy helping younger kids at my school and making sure they are safe," said Winsky. "Contributing my time and talents to help others is very important to me." In addition to his role as safety patrol captain, Winsky is a "wheelchair driver" and helps fellow students navigate the school's busy hallways and playground. Westmore has a unique population of special needs students because of its proximity to the Medical Center. To qualify as a driver, Winsky had to take a written test and a driving test—just like a real driver's license. He is also an avid ice skater and practices every morning before he comes to school. "Winsky is so organized that she developed and presented a contingency plan in case she was ever late for her safety patrol duty—it's been two years and she's never missed a day, but that plan is in place." Westmorn's safety patrol program emphasizes leadership and responsibility. Four teams of 12 students make up the safety patrol team and are recommended for the position by their teachers. According to West, there is a waiting list to join the patrol, because students know what an honor it is. Each year the safety patrol selects 10 outstanding school safety patrollers from schools throughout the state to receive the honor of being inducted into the School Safety Patrol Hall of Fame.

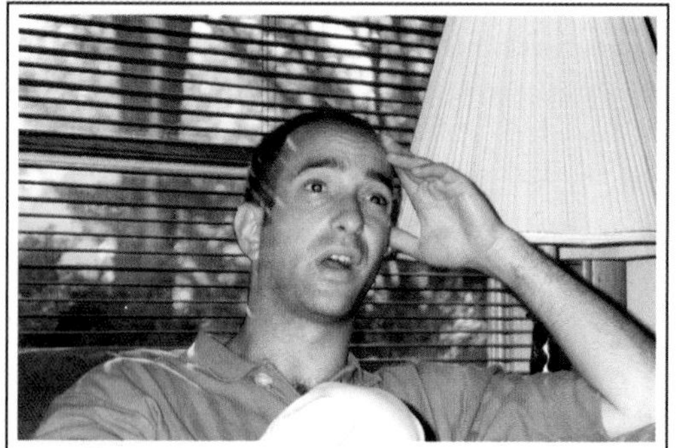

Bertrand Winsky interviewed about school safety

Westmore Middle School safety supervisor is interviewed by the shool safety council to discuss Winsky's exemplary conduct as the head of safety at the school.

That should give you an idea of how much care filmmakers put into their craft.

Winsky Honored

Bertrand Winsky

On a sunny morning in September, Bertrand was on duty near the school's entrance with his Patrol Advisor helping students cross the busy road in front of the school. As students were crossing, a small white car suddenly sped around a corner and towards a crossing fifth-grade girl. Bertrand quickly pushed the girl out of the way before the car flew by and quickly turned into the driveway of the school without any regard for the School Safety Patrol or students crossing the street in front of him.

After only two weeks at his School Safety Patrol post, Bertrand's quick thinking saved a kindergarten student. When the 5 year old's mother dropped him off for school, the kindergartener became extremely upset about her leaving. Not wanting to hold up traffic, the mother pulled forward and turned into a parking space. Bertrand spotted the crying young boy as he ran along the sidewalk following his mother's car. He ran after him and caught up to him right before he ran across the drive to his mother's parked car. Bertrand stopped the child from darting into the drive just as a truck was passing by. Several witnesses said the driver would likely have not seen the child nor had time to stop if the kindergartener had not been stopped by Winsky..

As North America's largest motoring and leisure travel organization, the safety program provides more than 51 million students with safety services. Since its founding in 1902, the not-for-profit, fully tax-paying safety patrol has been a leader and advocate for the safety and security of all travelers. safety patrol clubs can be visited on the Internet.

WINSKY NAMED SAFETY SUPERVISOR

On a sunny morning in September, Bertrand was on duty near the school's entrance with his Patrol Advisor helping students cross the busy road in front of the school. As students were crossing, a small white car suddenly sped around a corner and towards a crossing fifth-grade girl. Bertrand quickly pushed the girl out of the way before the car flew by and quickly turned into the driveway of the school without any regard for the School Safety Patrol or students crossing the street in front of him.

After only two weeks at his School Safety Patrol post, Bertrand's quick thinking saved a kindergarten student. When the 5 year old's mother dropped him off for school, the kindergartener became extremely upset about her leaving. Not wanting to hold up traffic, the mother pulled forward and turned into a parking space. Bertrand spotted the crying young boy as he ran along the sidewalk following his mother's car. He ran after him and caught up to him right before he ran across the drive to his mother's parked car. Bertrand stopped the child from darting into the drive just as a truck was passing by. Several witnesses said the driver would likely have not seen the child nor had time to stop if the kindergartener had not been stopped by Winsky..

As North America's largest motoring and leisure travel organization, the safety program provides more than 51 million students with safety services. Since its founding in 1902, the not-for-profit, fully tax-paying safety patrol has been a leader and advocate for the safety and security of all travelers. safety patrol clubs can be visited on the Internet.

There's a lot of work the set designers do that goes unnoticed by the audience, because it's in the background. But their work isn't just for the moviegoers to enjoy—it's for the actors, too. If the actors are in an environment that feels convincing, it helps them do their jobs better.

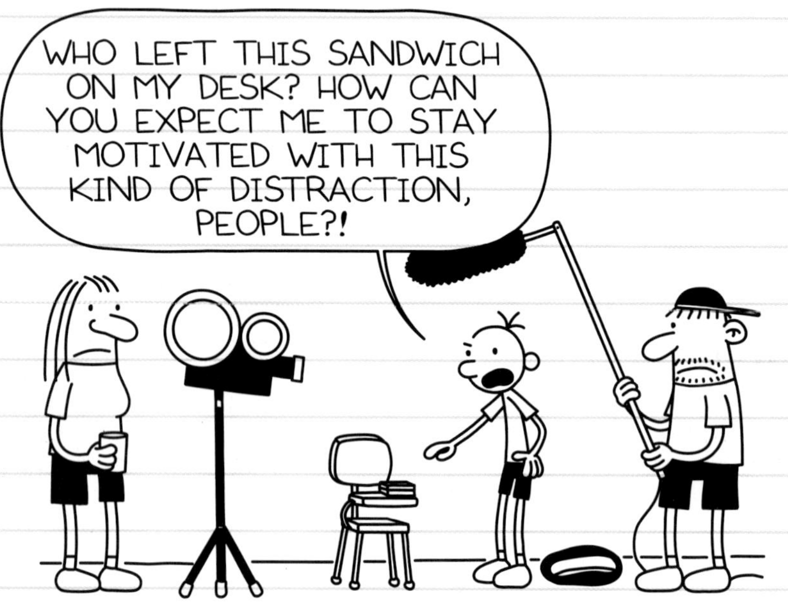

It's the set designers' job to make the audience believe that the environments in the film are real and not just some part of a movie set. But almost everything you see on the screen was created for the film.

Take Greg's homeroom, for example. It's loaded with all sorts of items you'd see in a typical classroom. But everything, from the textbooks on the shelves to the pencils and pens, was brought in from a prop warehouse.

ACTION!

Once all the pieces were in place, it was finally time to start filming. Each shot begins with the snap of a clapboard in front of the camera.

Sound and film are recorded separately in a movie, so the time stamp of the clapboard helps the filmmakers match up the sound and film later on.

The first scene shot was in Greg and Rowley's homeroom. Remember, a movie is usually filmed out of sequence, and this particular scene was from the middle of the story, when Greg comes to school and is horrified to discover he's wearing the same clothes as Rowley.

In fact, all the scenes that happen in the boys' homeroom were filmed on the first day. The kids changed outfits in between each scene.

The actors are surrounded by lots of people, cameras, and equipment, so it's kind of amazing that they can focus on delivering their lines.

Most people think filming is really exciting, but the truth is, it can be kind of boring. There's a lot of waiting around while the camera and lighting people set up their equipment for each shot. It can take as much as an hour just to put the cameras and lights in the right spot for a new scene.

And when filming actually begins, the same shot is filmed over and over again.

So even if an actor is saying a funny line, by the fourteenth take nobody really thinks it's that funny anymore.

TAKE ONE

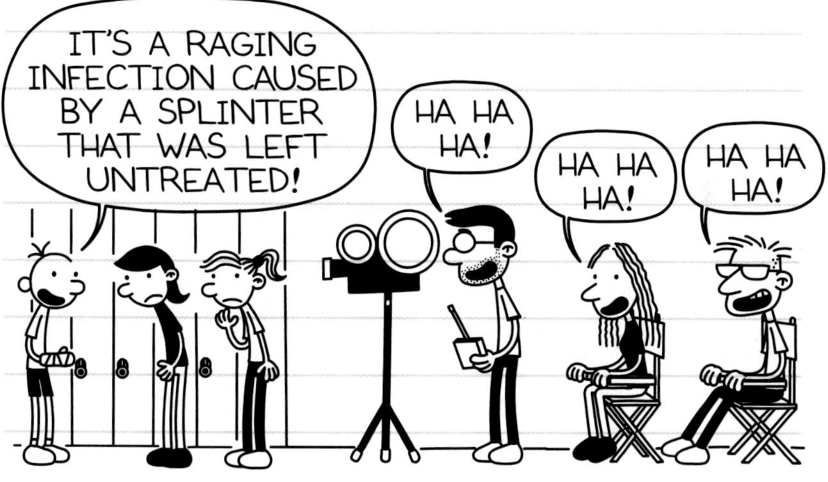

TAKE FOURTEEN

The reason the director films so many takes is to make sure he has lots of choices later on when the movie is put together. And even after a single scene is shot several times, the director then films the same one from a different angle to capture the other characters' reactions.

So filming takes a really long time. In fact, a whole DAY of filming usually produces only about two MINUTES of a finished movie.

Whenever there's a break in filming, the hair and makeup artists touch up the actors to get them ready for the next shot.

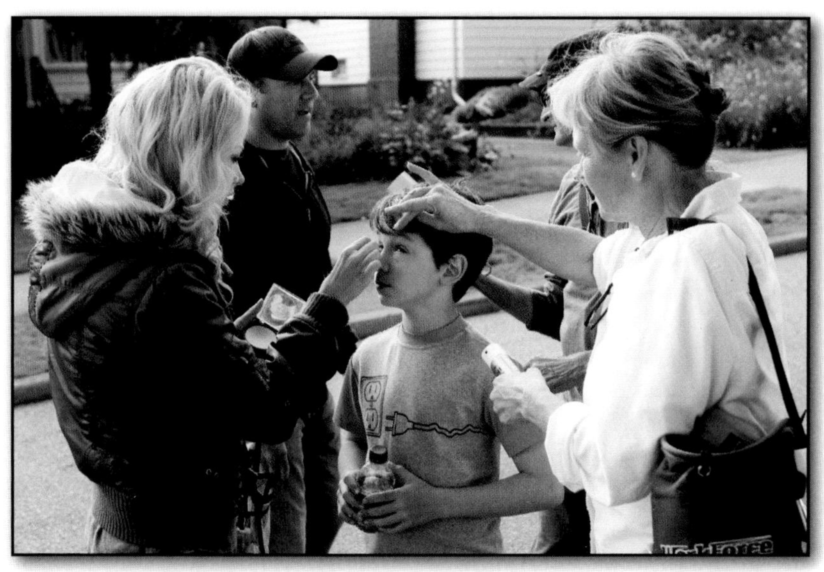

The actors need to look exactly the same for each take. A lot of time goes by between shots, and the actors' hair and makeup can get messed up. It's important that the actors look like they did in the last shot, or the audience is going to notice the difference.

One of the ways the hair and makeup artists keep track of how the actors look is by taking digital pictures of them after each take. That way there's a record that everyone can refer back to.

Sometimes a REALLY long time goes by between takes. An actor might film part of a scene one day, and then film another part of the same scene two months later. That's when the "continuity" pictures really come in handy.

For example, in one of the early outdoor scenes, Robert has zinc on his nose. Another part of the same scene was shot a month later, and the hair and makeup people were able to use the photos to get Robert's nose just right.

Hair is a real challenge, because it grows. The hairstylist has to make sure things don't get out of control during filming.

The actors have to get regular trims so their hair stays more or less the same length throughout the movie.

One of the toughest decisions the filmmakers had to make was how to style Zach's hair for the movie. Long meetings were held to discuss the issue, and everyone had a different opinion.

After a lot of experimentation and tons of hair gel, Zach's "wimpy sprigs" were created and the problem was solved.

The hair and makeup artists don't just make the actors look good. Sometimes it's their job to make them look BAD. In one case, the makeup artist needed to add fake pimples to an actor who didn't have any.

And in another, the hairstylist needed to figure out how to give a mullet to a teenager who had short hair.

A DAY IN THE LIFE

Every minute of an actor's day is scheduled ahead of time. Each morning, the actors get a call sheet that tells them what they'll be doing that day.

~~TOF~~ Vancouver Productions LTD - DWK

Diary of a Wimpy Kid

CREW CALL: 7:30am

DATE: Tues Sept 22, 2009

Producers: Nina Jacobson, Brad Simpson
Exec. Producer: Jeff Kinney
Co-Producer: Ethan Smith
Director: Thor Freudenthal
Production Manager: Warren Carr
1st AD: Pete Whyte

Breakfast Call: 6:30a
Shooting Call: 9:00a
Lunch Call: 1:30p
Day: 28 of 45
Sunrise: 6:49a **Sunset:** 7:09p
WEATHER: Sunny 23c

DIRECTOR'S PICK UP: 6:35am

EPK ON SET TODAY (see below)

ALL VISITORS TO SET MUST BE PRE-APPROVED BY THE PRODUCTION MANAGER
NO PHOTOGRAPHY ALLOWED ON SET – EXCEPT THOSE CREW MEMBERS REQUIRING CONTINUITY SHOTS

Sc.	SET DESCRIPTION	D/N	Pgs	CAST	BG	LOCATION
151pt	INT. SCHOOL AUDITORIUM / STAGE Trees are on, Greg sees his family, Collin, Rowley & Rodrick	N22	7/8	1,8,11,12,36,43,46, 59, 63, 65		**Templeton School** **727 Templeton Drive** **Vancouver, BC** **(off Nanaimo & Adanac)**
152pt	INT. SCHOOL AUDITORIUM / STAGE Trees have stopped singing, Patty is yelling, Apple Fight!	N22	6/8	1,8,11,12,36,43,46, 59, 63, 65, 100,201,211		**CREW PARK** **Hastings Community Centre at 3000 Block East Pender Street**
153	INT. SCHOOL FOYER Susan & Frank meet up with Greg after the play	N22	3/8	1, 3, 4, 5, 25		**SHUTTLE TO...** **Catering & Work Trucks are on the School Lot**
	STILLS: Most Talented Yearbook Photo Additional 'After' Yearbook Photos					
	Total Page Count		2 0/8			

NO FORCED CALLS WITHOUT PRODUCTION MANAGER APPROVAL

#	CAST		CHARACTER	status	P/UP	HMW	SET	Notes:
1	Zach Gordon	K	Greg Heffley	W	8:00a	8:30a	9:00a	
2	Robert Capron	K	Rowley Jefferson	H	10:00a	-	-	← Tutoring Only at Set
3	Rachael Harris		Susan Heffley	PW	11:00a	11:30a	3:00p	← EPK Interview at 1:00pm
4	Steve Zahn		Frank Heffley	PW	11:00a	11:30a	3:00p	← EPK Interview at 12:30pm
5	Connor, Owen Fielding	K	Manny	SW	-	2:30p	3:00p	
6	Devon Bostick		Rodrick	T/F	travel	memo	#87	← See note below for 2nd p/up
8	Karan Brar	K	Chirag Gupta	W	10:00a	10:30a	11:00a	
11	Laine MacNeil	K	Patty Farrell	W	-	10:30a	11:00a	**NOTE TO ALL**
12	Jake D. Smith	K	Archie Kelly	W	-	8:30a	9:00a	
25	Shane Briscoe		Funny Dad	SW	-	1:00p	3:00p	**PLEASE USE CREW PARK.**
36	Adom Osei	K	Marty Porter	W	-	8:30a	9:00a	
43	Belita Moreno		Mrs. Norton	W	7:00a	7:30a	9:00a	
46	Ryan Grantham	K	Rodney James	W	-	8:30a	9:00a	**DO NOT PARK AT OR AROUND TEMPLETON SCHOOL.**
59	Jay Sidhu	K	Scarecrow / Singer 2	W	-	9:30a	10:00a	
63	Haris Cash	K	Tin Man / Singer 6	W	-	9:30a	10:00a	
65	Mariah Crupo	K	Good Witch / Singer 7	W	-	9:30a	10:00a	
100	Dave Hospes		Stunt Coordinator	W	-	-	7:30a	
201	Matt Phillips		Greg Stunt Double	SWF	-	9:00a	10:30a	
211	Marny Eng		Patty Farrell Stunt Double	SWF	-	9:00a	10:30a	

STAND INS:		
Utility 'Child' Stand In – Kevin Sloan	Call Time:	7:30a
Utility 'Child' Stand In – Bruce Creighton	Call Time:	7:30a
Utility 'Adult Female' Stand In – Bita Valentine	Call Time:	7:30a
Utility 'Adult Male' Stand In – (name tba)	Call Time:	12:30p

Please check with costumes daily regarding costume colour matches for characters playing

BACKGROUND PERFORMERS	CALL	SET	Notes:
ALL AUDIENCE BG TO COME WITH HAIR/MAKE UP/ WARDROBE COMPLETE APPRORIATE FOR A MIDDLE SCHOOL PLAY			
Audience Adults x 50, Music Teacher x 1, Audience Teens x 15	9:00a	10:00a	**Park in Crew Park, Shuttle to Holding Tents at Templeton**
Continuity Bad Witch x 1, Lion x 1, Stage Hands x 3, DJ/Stage Manager x 1	9:30a	10:00a	
Photo Doubles: #1. Greg, #12. Archie, #36. Marty, #46. Rodney	12:00	tba	
76 BG/Dbls + 25 Guardians = 101 Total			

DAILY DEPARTMENTAL NOTES

SAFETY MEETING and YOUNG & NEW WORKER ORIENTATION HELD ON SET AT CREW CALL

WEEKEND ACTIVITIES
Mon Sept 21 - Travel In: Jeff Kinney, Rachael Harris, Steve Zahn
Costume Fitting: 3:00pm - Rachael Harris w/ Monique at the hotel
Manny Meet'n Greet: 4:30pm – Rachael Harris with Owen & Connor Fielding at the hotel
Tutoring: Zach Gordon / as per Natalie & Linda Gordon

Film Break required at lunch.
Dailies at lunch.

SHOW & TELL: Rowley's Clothes (for Sc. 66 on Thursday)

EPK/MEDIA ON SET TODAY: Beth Goodwin, Troy Gross (Cartoon Network), Jason Wells +5 Execs (Abrams Publicity)
Josh Berger, Mateo di Lorio, Millar Montgomery for Interviews with Rachael Harris & Steve Zahn prior to shooting, Robert Capron after his school
Mike George (Fox) Marketing Shoot in School Room 223 for Cheese Touch Interactive Video with Robert Capron & Devon Bostick

LOCATIONS: Parking spot at the school needed for Jane Fielding and the 'Manny' twins, 4 Mirrors required in Extras Holding

Kids are only allowed to work seven and a half hours a day by law, so it doesn't make a lot of sense to have them sitting around while the camera and lighting crews set up a shot.

There are a few ways to keep things moving without having the actors waiting on set. One is to use adult stand-ins, or lighting doubles. Stand-ins take the kids' places so the camera and lighting people can get things just right, and then the kids are brought back in when the shot is ready. Stand-ins are usually the same general size as the kids they're doubling for.

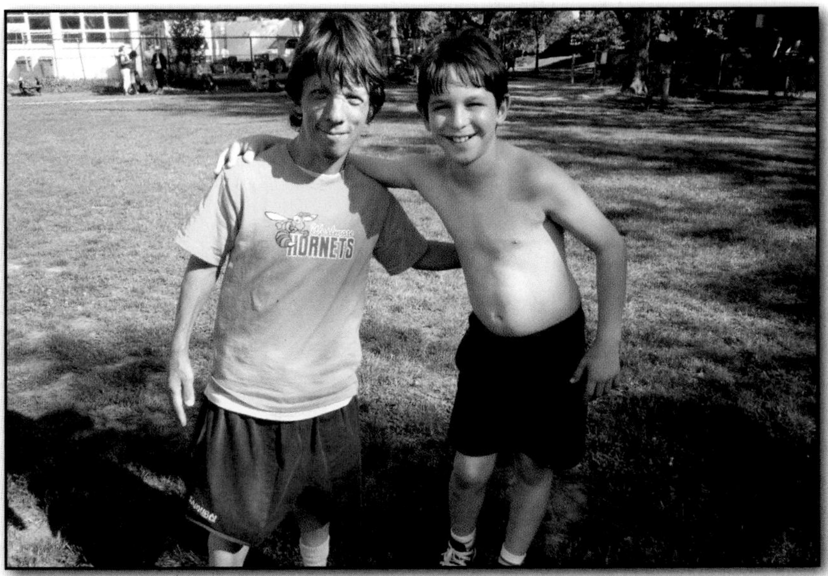

Another trick for keeping under the seven-and-a-half-hour time limit is to use doubles who are actually kids.

Let's say that Zach is in a scene with Robert, and the two actors are talking to each other. Well, when Robert's face is being shown on the camera, a double might be used for Zach, with only the back of the stand-in's head showing.

Meanwhile, Zach can be off in his trailer, taking a nap. As long as the double looks like the actor from behind, the audience won't notice.

Kids also have to spend at least fifteen hours a week going to school. Actors don't get a free pass just because they're working on a movie.

A special school was created inside a trailer so the actors in the "Diary of a Wimpy Kid" movie could keep up with their classmates back home. A set teacher tutored each kid individually to make sure the actors didn't fall behind in their education.

What's ironic is that both Robert and Zach were missing their real-life first days of middle school because they were playing characters entering middle school in a movie.

Usually, the kids do their schoolwork in the classroom trailer, but when it's nice outside, they set up wherever they can find a comfortable place to work.

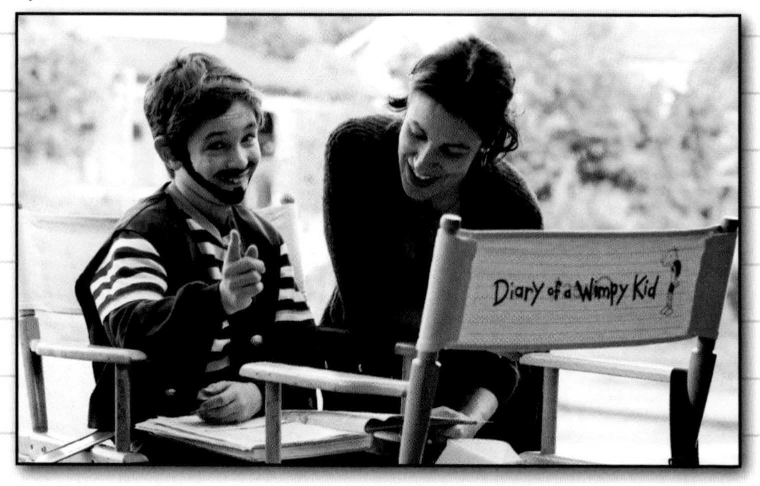

The kids don't usually go to school in long chunks of time— they study whenever there's a break in filming.

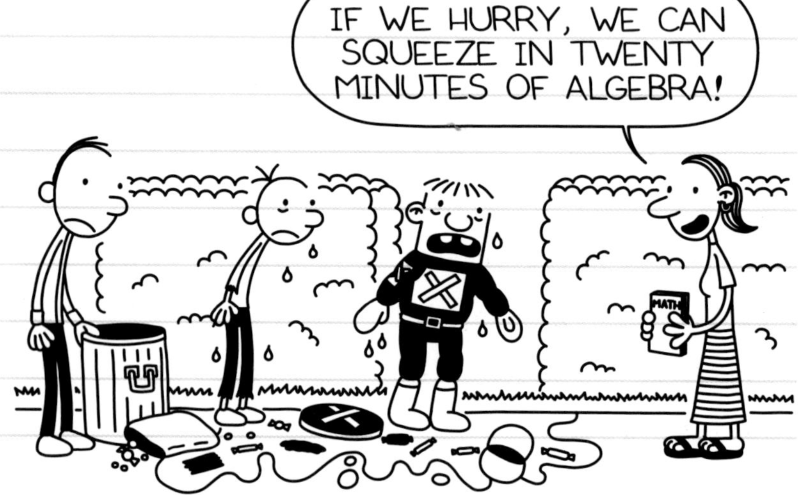

On top of regular schoolwork, the kids get to go on field trips and get some phys ed, just like their classmates back home.

So where do actors go when they're not on the set acting or doing school stuff? They go to the "circus." The circus is the big group of trailers where each actor has a place to wind down.

The trailers are like rooms on wheels. The reason the actors are set up in trailers is because when the crew needs to go to a new shooting location, the trailers move with them.

The trailers are nice inside—many are equipped with a flat-screen TV with surround sound, a desk, a refrigerator, a bathroom, and a big leather couch.

Here's Zach Gordon stepping into his trailer for the first time—

The size of an actor's trailer usually depends on how big their part in the movie is. If an actor has a lead role, chances are they get a big trailer.

If an actor has a small part in the film, well, their accommodations might not be as roomy.

The trailers aren't just for actors. The producers, director, and many of the other people working on the film have trailers too.

Plus, the wardrobe department, the propmaster, and the makeup crew all have "office space" in their trailers where they can do their work.

The actors get a break in the middle of the day for lunch. The catering trailer is basically a restaurant on wheels.

The people who make the food change the menu each day to keep things fresh. But that doesn't stop the crew from giving them a hard time.

The whole cast eats together, and sometimes that can be a little strange.

Besides lunch, there are always snacks available in an area called "craft service." That's where actors can snack on hot chocolate, beef jerky, peanuts, bagels, crackers, and lots of other stuff.

The craft service area on the "Diary of a Wimpy Kid" set was mostly sugar-free, because kids tend to work better when they're focused.

When the cast is done for the day, they go back to their hotel. The actors stayed in large suites in downtown Vancouver that were meant to make them feel at home. The suites had two bedrooms, a family room, a dining room, and a kitchen.

Zach's favorite thing to do in his downtime was to hang out with his mom and play video games—sometimes at the same time.

Robert and his dad watched almost every movie in the James Bond series.

Sometimes the actors hung out with each other at the hotel pool, where they could have fun and just enjoy being kids.

The great thing about living in a hotel is that you don't have to make your bed or clean up after yourself. But after three months of living like kings, it was a little hard for the kids to adjust once they got back home.

I'D LIKE YOU TO PICK UP YOUR SOCKS.
DON'T WE HAVE PEOPLE WHO CAN DO THAT?

The actors' parents aren't the only ones looking out for them. Everyone on the set acts as an extended family and helps support the kids during filming.

The kids are also assigned acting coaches who help steer them through the sometimes chaotic world of moviemaking.

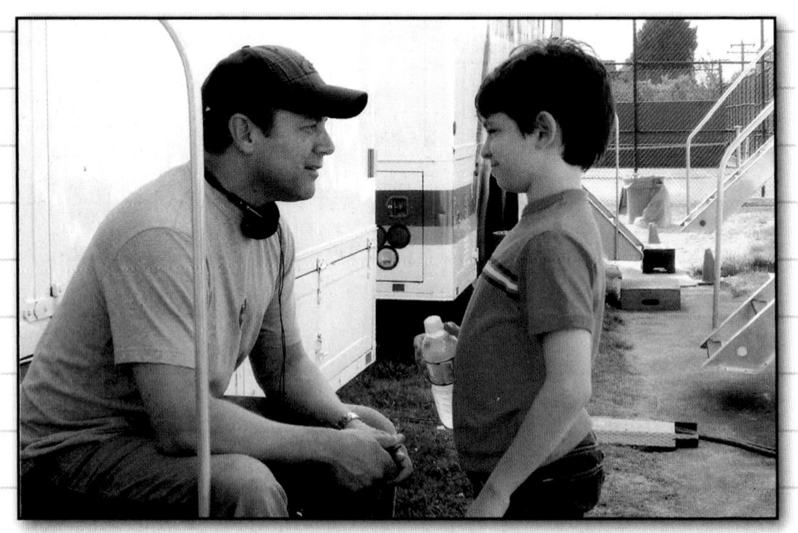

It's the acting coach's job to help the kids memorize their lines, but they do much more than that. The coaches make sure the kids are eating right so they can keep their energy level up, and they try to balance the work with plenty of fun for the actors.

The acting coaches are with the kids from the beginning of their day until the end. Since "Diary of a Wimpy Kid" was shot out of order, it was important for the kids to be reminded of what happened in the scene before the one they were about to perform. The acting coach goes through the day's scenes on the early-morning car ride from the hotel to the set.

IN THIS SCENE RODRICK JUST WOKE YOU UP, SO YOU NEED TO ACT TIRED AND GRUMPY.
I THINK I CAN HANDLE THAT.

The coaches for "Diary of a Wimpy Kid" were actors with years of television and film experience, so they were especially prepared to help the kids navigate through the whole process.

One of the acting coaches actually had a role in the movie as Mrs. Norton, the drama teacher.

EXTRA INGREDIENTS

Now you know what a typical day is like for the main actors, but what about those people you see walking through the background of a scene?

Those people are called "extras," and it's their job to fill out a scene so it feels real. Extras don't have any spoken lines, but the work they do is very important.

Extras are usually people who want to get involved in moviemaking or are just looking for something fun and interesting to do for a few days. They get to be a part of a movie, and they get paid, too.

But being an extra is hard work. The hours can be long, with lots and lots of waiting between filming. Extras don't get trailers like the rest of the actors, so they have to find whatever spot's available during their downtime.

But it's all worth it when they get to see their big moment play out on the screen.

PAGE TO SCREEN

Here's how a few of the drawings from the book translated to scenes in the movie.

Cartooning is the art of boiling something down to its simplest parts, but in a movie, a director is working on a much bigger canvas and needs to "fill out the frame" with lots of detail.

TWEET!

FIGHT!

One of the more complicated scenes to film was when Greg and Rowley get into a fight and the teenagers show up on the playground.

Here's how the director storyboarded the scene—

And here's how things looked in real life—

A REAL PRODUCTION

One scene that really shows the difference between writing a book and making a movie is the school play. In order to create a play in a book, all you have to do is draw a few doodles and write down a paragraph or two to describe the scene. Easy, right? Well, creating a school play in a film is a whole different matter.

To stage "The Wonderful Wizard of Oz" for the movie, the wardrobe department needed to create a costume for every kid, lights had to be rigged, sets had to be designed and painted, and a choreographer had to plan out how and where the actors moved.

In other words, everything that goes into putting on a REAL play had to be done for the school play in the movie.

Of course, the play couldn't look TOO professional, or it wouldn't look like it was put on by kids. So everything had to have that middle school touch. For example, the trunks of the costumes for the three trees were made of styrofoam, and the branches were swimming pool noodles.

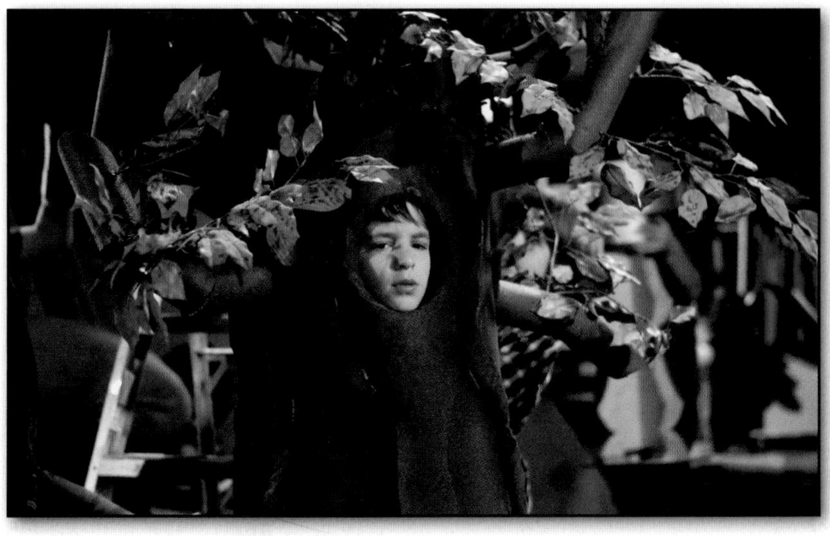

Some of the other costumes were a little more complicated and were created by the wardrobe department.

The costumes for the school play needed to look different from the ones in the "Wizard of Oz" movie, so the wardrobe department put a lot of work into making the costumes unique.

The costume designers researched the types of fabric that were worn when "The Wonderful Wizard of Oz" book was written and used those for the play.

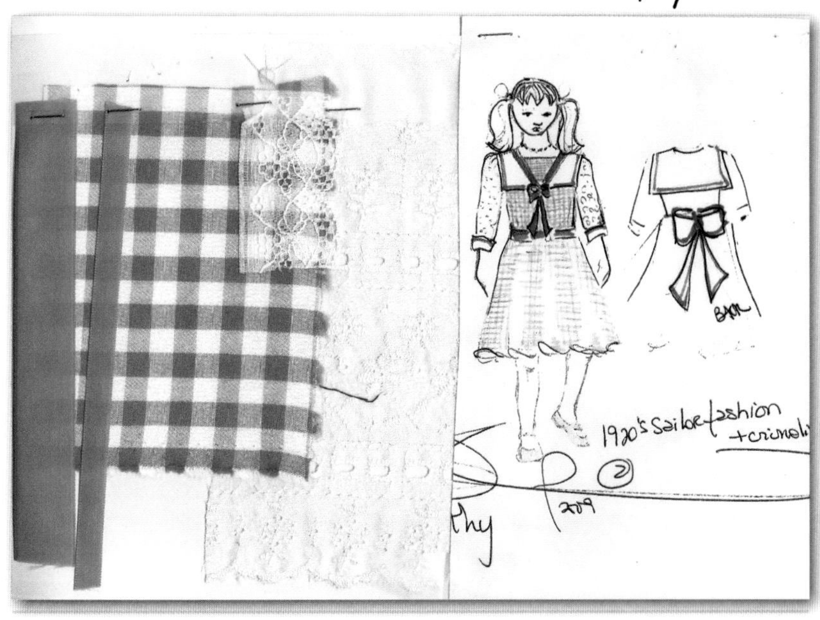

Finally, the actors got to try on their costumes.

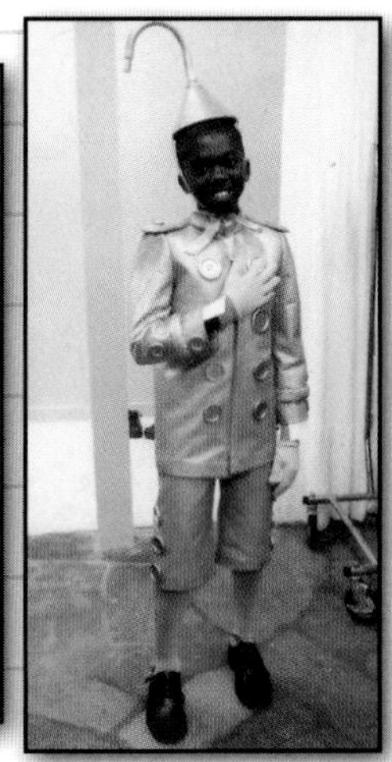

In the book, Greg has to sing a song called "We Three Trees." A songwriter had to compose music for the song, which you can hear in the movie.

And to give you an idea of how far the art department went to create a convincing school play, they even designed playbills and handed them out to the audience members.

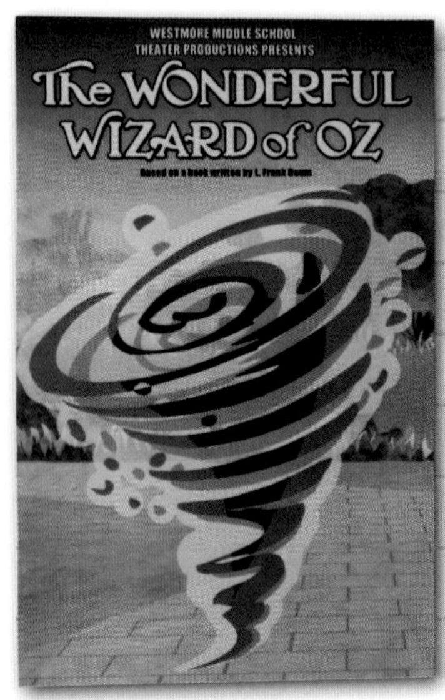

WESTMORE MIDDLE SCHOOL
THEATER PRODUCTIONS PRESENTS
The WONDERFUL WIZARD of OZ
Based on a book written by L. Frank Baum

Speaking of those audience members, it took a few hundred extras to fill up the auditorium.

It was the biggest "set piece" in the movie and took three days to film.

One of the toughest scenes to shoot was in the middle of the school play. In the book, Manny yells out Greg's nickname when the curtains first open.

It may be easy to make that happen on paper, but it turns out it's not so easy to pull off in real life.

The school play was one of the first scenes for the twins playing Manny, and they weren't really on board with the whole "acting" thing yet.

In fact, they didn't seem to know what to think when they were suddenly a part of a new "family" in a big auditorium filled with strangers and with lights and cameras pointed at them.

Luckily, the filmmakers figured out the secret to winning the twins over: candy.

Each twin took turns playing Manny during the scene. One of the producers stood in front of the kids and yelled "Bubby" repeatedly, hoping Owen or Connor would copy him.

Owen caught on, shouting ten perfect "Bubbys" in a row. Afterward, both twins were rewarded with a handful of Tootsie Rolls for their efforts.

Sometimes moviemaking is about capturing a big explosion or dramatic moment on film, but for "Diary of a Wimpy Kid," the high point came when a three-year-old actor delivered his line.

HEY, THAT WASN'T IN THE BOOK!

One of the other big set pieces in the movie, the Mother-Son Sweetheart Dance, wasn't in the book. So why was the scene written for the film?

Well, sometimes you need to create some extra emotional firepower to help tell a story. In the book, Greg and Rowley have a falling-out, and things slowly build until they get into a fistfight.

That happens in the movie, too. But the writers felt like there needed to be an extra spark to push the boys over the edge. So the Mother-Son Sweetheart Dance was created to show how things reach a boiling point.

By the time Greg and Rowley meet up at the dance, they haven't been friends for a while. Rowley's found a replacement in his new best friend, Collin.

When Greg sees Rowley, he tries to reconnect with him, only to get shot down.

Like most of the boys at the dance, Greg doesn't want to be there. But Rowley's a different story. He's excited to be at the dance with his mom, and they've been rehearsing their moves at home.

So when their special song plays, they hit the dance floor.

Greg is happy to see his ex-friend make a fool out of himself. But then, to Greg's shock, the crowd gets into it, and Rowley and his mom become the stars of the dance.

Greg watches in horror as the whole scene unfolds. And when Greg and Rowley run into each other on the blacktop the next day, Greg is itching for a fight.

Creating the Mother-Son Sweetheart Dance was just as complicated as staging the school play. The set designers had to decorate a gym with balloons, streamers, posters, and a disco ball.

About two hundred extras were brought in to play the mother-son pairs. Most of the people you see in the scene are real-life moms and their kids. And with all those boys and their moms dressed up, it was just as awkward as the real thing.

The woman playing Rowley's mother isn't an actress—she's Robert's mom in real life. The two of them rehearsed their dance routine with a professional choreographer for about a week.

To give you an idea of how something that looks simple can actually be complicated, take the scene where Collin hands Rowley an ice cream cone. In the movie, it looks like this—

No big deal, right? Well, believe it or not, it was one of the hardest scenes to film.

First of all, it was hot in the gym where the dance was filmed, so you couldn't have ice cream sitting out without melting. The ice cream was kept in a freezer in a kitchen about one hundred feet away. When the director yelled "Action!" a prop man started making two ice cream cones as fast as he could.

Then he ran the cones out to the actors and handed them off at the exact moment Collin came into the scene.

The actors each took a single lick of their ice cream, then handed the cones back to the prop guy, who took them back to the kitchen to throw them away.

This went on for half an hour, and by the time the scene was finished, there was a trash can in the kitchen full of once-licked ice cream cones.

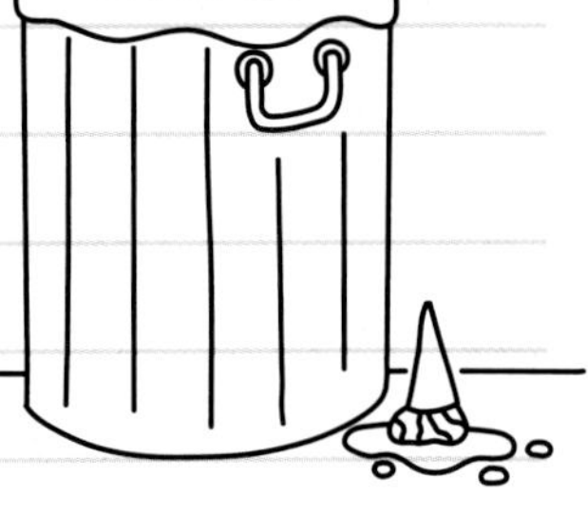

That's something you'll only see on a movie set.

AN AWESOME VIDEO

Most of the time, filmmakers strive to do their best work. But every once in a while they get to have a little fun and lower their standards.

In the "Diary of a Wimpy Kid" movie, there's a video shown in the classroom called "It's Awesome to Be Me." It's one of those outdated videos that they show in school year after year.

The filmmakers had a lot of fun shooting a very corny, unpolished video that looked like it was made thirty years ago. The actors in the video had to wear hairstyles and clothes from the 1980s.

In the video, a teen learns that if he just acts cool, people will like him. So he break-dances in the library, impressing everyone and winning new friends.

The whole scene was filmed with a video camera to make it look like it was created a long time ago.

DOUBLE TAKE

Since "Diary of a Wimpy Kid" doesn't have a lot of over-the-top action scenes, you might not think that special effects play much of a role in the movie. But they're actually used a lot.

A special effect is any kind of visual trick a filmmaker uses to create an illusion. One of the most common special effects is replacing an actor with a stunt double.

When you're filming something that might be dangerous, you usually replace the actor with an experienced stunt double who knows how to perform a scene without getting hurt. For the stunt double to be convincing, they have to be more or less the same size as the actor they're replacing.

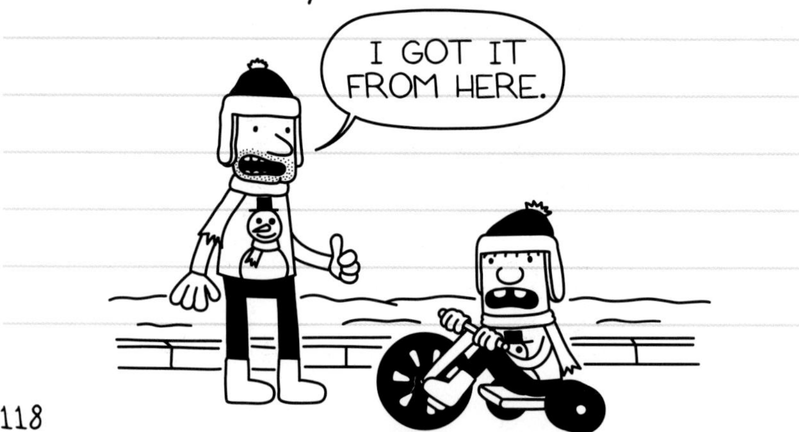

Usually, when a stunt double is used, they're filmed from far away so the audience can't tell. In the scene where Patty Farrell tackles Greg at the end of the school play, TWO stunt doubles were used—one for Patty and one for Greg.

Sometimes, in scenes where the actors are filmed close up, you can't get away with using a stunt double, and the actors have to do their own stunts. For the wrestling scene between Fregley and Greg, the actors were trained by a professional.

Some stunts are complicated and take a lot of planning. One scene that took some serious work was where Rowley gets knocked off his Big Wheel by Greg's football.

In the movie, Greg throws a football at Rowley as he's speeding down the hill. But when the scene was filmed, Zach didn't throw anything—he just pretended to.

The football was added later on as a visual effect.

When the football connects with the Big Wheel, Rowley goes flying. During filming, Robert was replaced by an adult stunt double. The front wheel of the bike was connected to a cable, which was attached to a stationary object. When the cable went taut, the stunt double went flying.

The stuntman was wearing padding underneath his clothes. And because he was a trained professional, he knew how to land without getting hurt.

You might've noticed the giant blue backdrop behind the stunt double. The backdrop is called a "blue screen," and it's another tool filmmakers use to twist reality. Here's how it works: An actor is filmed performing in front of a giant blue sheet, or "traveling matte."

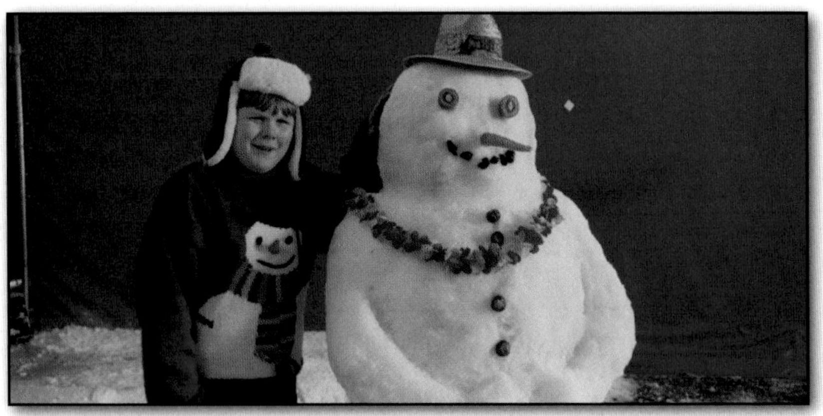

Another shot, called a "background plate," is created separately.

Then the two shots come together in a "composite." The blue color is removed, and the background plate can be seen underneath.

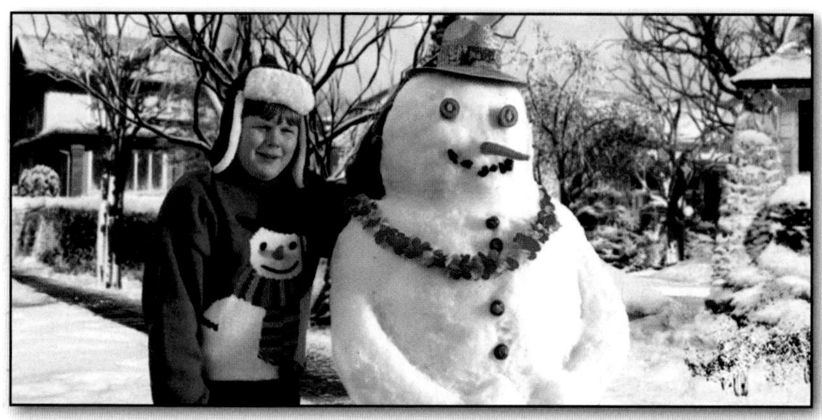

This technique is used whenever it's not practical to film the actors in a specific location or during a certain time of year. Since "Diary of a Wimpy Kid" was filmed in the summer and early fall, the filmmakers had to create their own winter scenes. This image of the Heffley house was created with a mixture of a real photo and some computer artistry.

A blue screen was also used to film one of Greg's fantasies, when he imagines himself as a wealthy adult. It was easier to film the actors in front of a blue screen than to fly them out to shoot the scene in front of a real mansion.

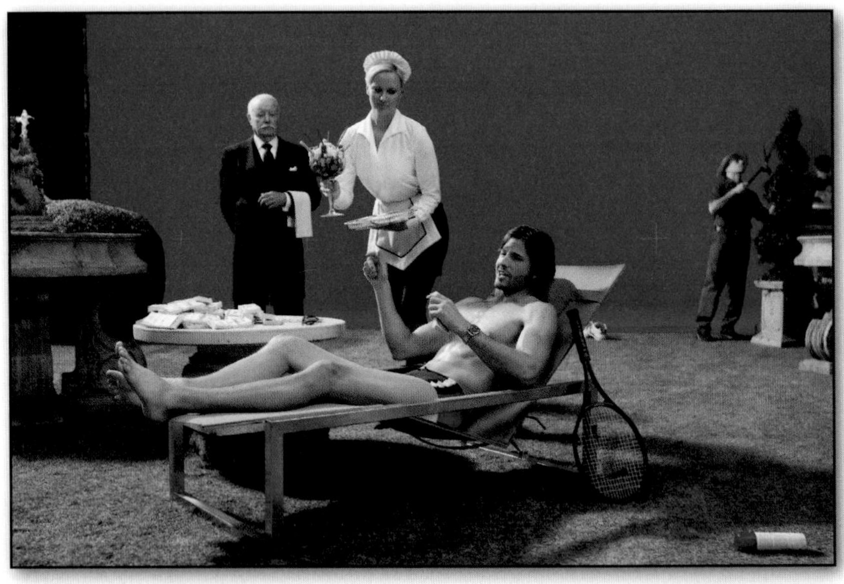

Sometimes a blue screen is used to re-create something that's already been filmed. There's a scene in the movie where Chirag tells Greg and Rowley the story behind the Cheese. A few weeks after the original scene was shot, the director decided he wanted to get another few takes. But the school and the extras from the original scene weren't available anymore.

So the director used a blue screen and shot the actors in the foreground, then combined the new foreground image with the old background image. And if it wasn't pointed out, you'd never notice.

Sometimes filming against a fake background isn't enough to convince the audience that a scene is real. If you have a snow scene, you've gotta have snow in the foreground, too. So the filmmakers had to make it snow in September.

Here's how they did it. First they laid a thick white sheet of plastic down on the ground to cover the green grass. Then they used a "snow hopper" and a giant hose to blow the fake snow onto the ground and into the trees and bushes.

The fake snow was made of paper. It looks almost exactly like real snow. You can even make snow angels in it if you want.

The only downside to the fake snow is that it had to be cleaned up afterward—you can't just roll into someone's neighborhood and leave a couple hundred pounds of white paper behind.

In order to make it look like the boys had spent the day out in the snow, blush was put on their ears, noses, and cheeks.

Snow wasn't the only kind of weather that had to be created for the movie. One of the scenes called for a downpour, and you can't fake rain with chopped-up paper.

You might remember a scene from the book where Greg chases some kindergartners with a worm on a stick.

Well, the writers decided that Greg had to do something worse in the movie than chase kids with a worm. So they created a scene where Greg is walking the kindergartners home and he thinks he sees the teenagers who chased him and Rowley on Halloween night. So Greg hides the kindergartners—and himself—in a dug-out hole on a construction site.

And all this happens during a rainstorm.

The filmmakers set up a giant crane and used a fire hose to create rain on a sunny day.

All the cameras and equipment had to be protected from the downpour with plastic. The kids had to be protected, too. Each one wore a wet suit underneath their clothes so they didn't get too cold.

The weather isn't the only thing the filmmakers can fake. They can even manipulate the time of day.

Shooting outdoors can be a challenge, because as the sun goes down, the light changes. But the lighting department has all sorts of filters, bulbs, and reflectors to make it look like a bright, sunny afternoon, even if it's not. In fact, just about any type of lighting condition can be simulated by the filmmakers.

Sometimes the time of day needs to be tweaked even more drastically. When it does, the filmmakers can change night to day or day to night.

One nighttime Halloween scene needed to be shot in the middle of the afternoon. So the crew covered the entire front of the house with black cloth, which is called "tenting." When you see the scene in the movie, you'll swear it was filmed at night.

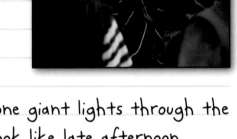

Another scene was filmed at night, but had to look like it was shot in the day. So the lighting crew shone giant lights through the windows to make it look like late afternoon.

TAKING OVER

Most of "Diary of a Wimpy Kid" was filmed "on location" in real schools, stores, and neighborhoods in the Vancouver area. This helped give the movie a realistic feel that might've been missing if it was all filmed on a Hollywood set.

So what happens when a film crew wants to make a movie in a real neighborhood?

The filmmakers strike a deal with the residents that allows the movie crew to shoot in their neighborhood for a certain amount of time and under certain conditions. Most people are excited to have their neighborhood included in a movie, so it usually works out pretty smoothly.

Some people even offer up their homes for filming. Three of the houses in the "Diary of a Wimpy Kid" movie—Greg's house, Rowley's house, and Fregley's house—were real homes that people actually lived in.

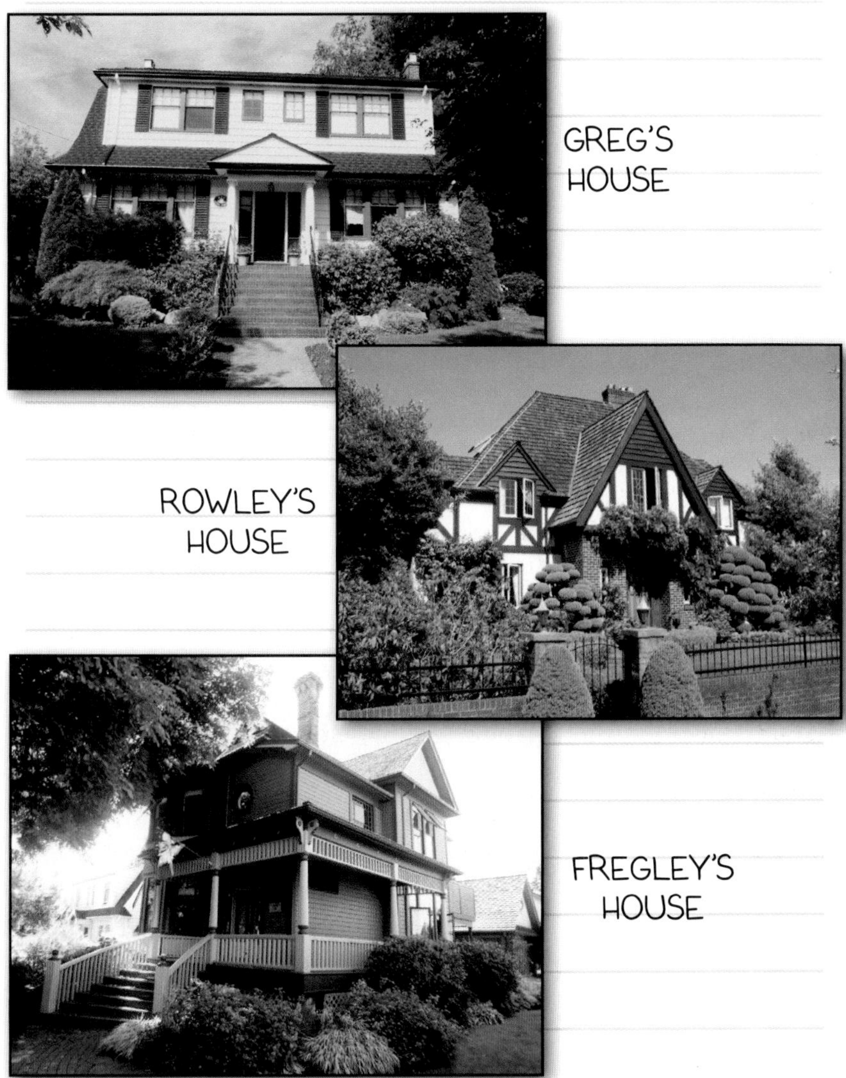

GREG'S HOUSE

ROWLEY'S HOUSE

FREGLEY'S HOUSE

The residents let the movie crew into their homes and find other places to stay during filming.

Of course when the film crew moves in, they make a lot of changes. First of all, everything that isn't nailed down — pictures, lamps, even furniture — is removed and stored someplace else.

Next, the set designers and decorators bring in stuff to make it look like the fictional characters live there. Everything from the pictures hanging on the walls to the books on the shelves helps make it feel believable.

For example, Greg's dad is a Civil War buff in the book, so in the movie the Heffley home is full of Civil War books and miniature figurines.

To really make the homes authentic, the set designers asked for family photos of the actors so they could be placed on walls and on dresser tops. Some pictures in Rowley's room came from the Caprons' family photo album.

Just as costumes tell you something about the characters, so do the homes they live in.

Take a look at Rowley's room. You can see that he's into dinosaurs and astronauts, and that his tastes are a little young for his age.

Even the knobs on Rowley's dresser drawers are astronaut-themed.

You get the feeling that Rowley's mom had a heavy hand in decorating her son's bedroom.

In the books, Rowley is a big fan of teen singing sensation Joshie. So the art department created some Joshie posters for Rowley's room.

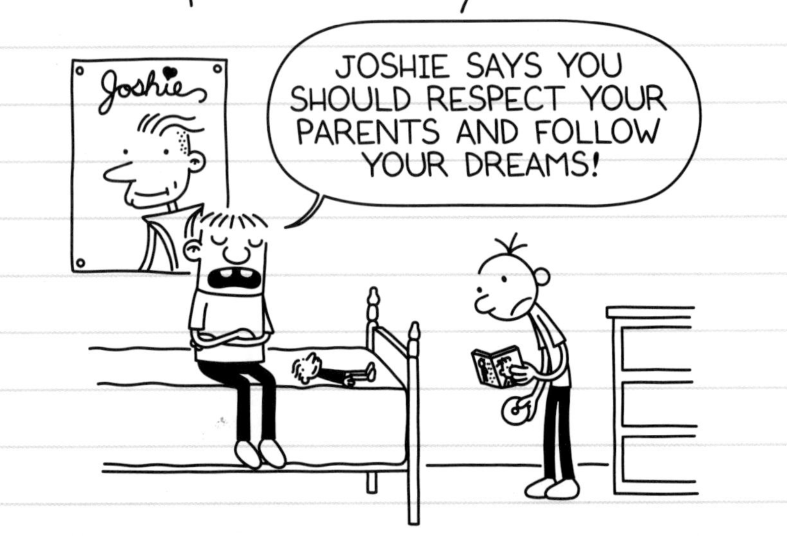

The art department designed everything in Rowley's room, from the wallpaper to his bed. They wanted to make his bed look childish and cool at the same time.

Here are the plans that were drawn up to make Rowley's rocket bed.

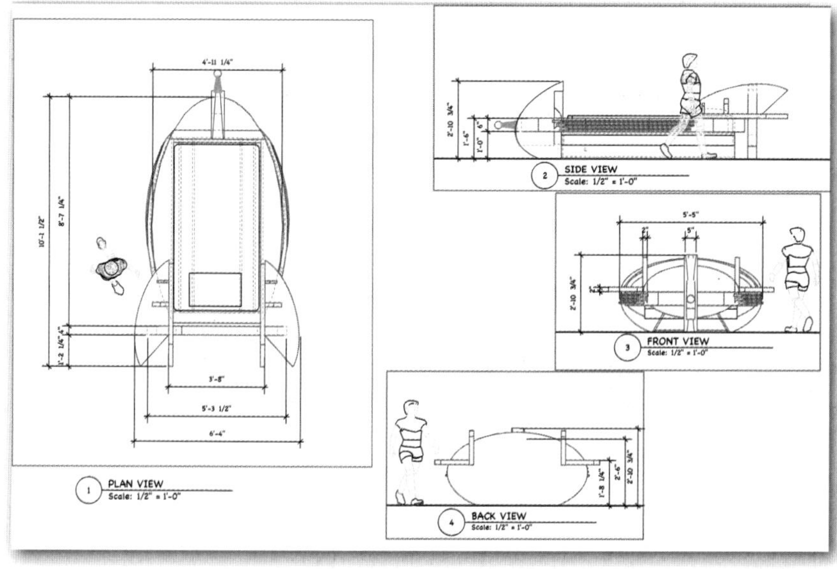

All this work was done to give you a feeling for the kind of person Rowley is. And it was all created for a handful of scenes that last only a minute or two in the finished movie.

Fregley's room tells a different story. From the pictures on the walls to the strange items on his shelves, it's clear Fregley isn't your typical middle school kid.

You get the sense that Fregley doesn't have many friends. Everything in his room is designed to make you feel uneasy—just the way Greg feels after he steps into Fregley's house for a sleepover.

Fregley's living room, where his mom makes clothes (and maybe even playmates), was also designed to make you share Greg's discomfort.

FAKING IT

There are some items you see in scenes that can't be purchased — they have to be made just for the movie. The person who creates these items is called a "propmaster."

The propmaster made dozens of objects for the film. He made the tree costumes for the play and the safety patrol badges. He made all the strange items sitting on Fregley's shelves, from the dung beetles to the scab collection.

He even made the booger stuck to the note Fregley hands to Greg. And for the record, it was made of a sticky adhesive product mixed with tinted wax.

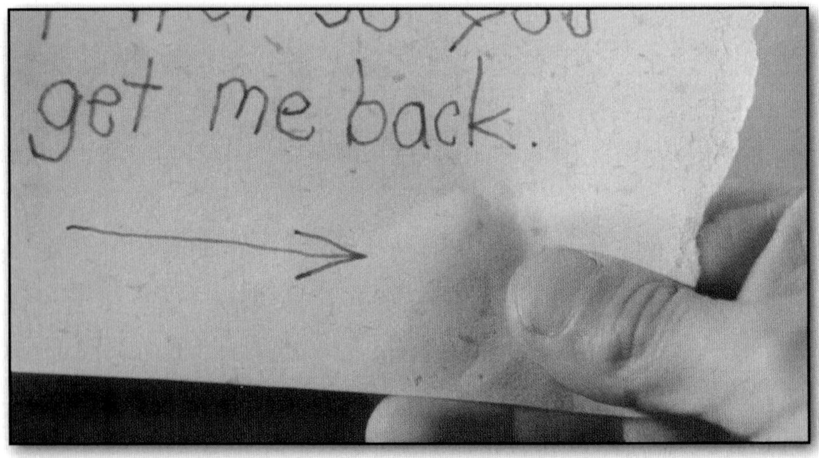

One of the most complicated items the propmaster made was Greg's diary. The cover of the "Diary of a Wimpy Kid" book you see in stores was designed on a computer, but for the movie the propmaster had to create a real book, cover and all.

It took weeks to make the journal seen in the film. The propmaster needed to find all the materials to create a real journal and bind them together. The stitching on the cover of the "Diary of a Wimpy Kid" book might be digital, but in the movie it's the real thing.

In the movie, Rowley breaks his arm. Over time, more and more people sign his cast at school.

Several rubber casts were created to show the passage of time in the film. They all had a seam in the back so Robert could easily put them on and take them off.

The propmaster drew signatures on little slips of paper and stuck them to the cast for positioning, then copied them onto the rubber by hand to create the fully covered version. Then he made two more copies of that one, just in case.

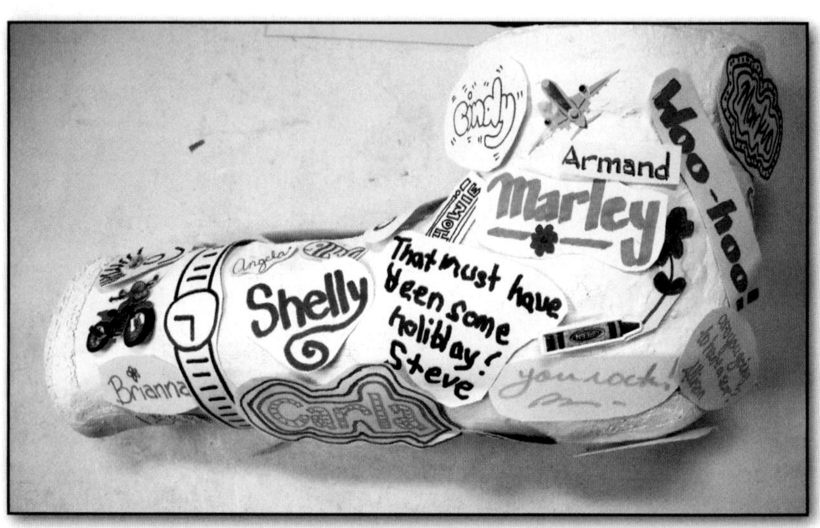

For the earlier version of the cast, the propmaster simply used fewer signatures, making sure to keep them in the right position.

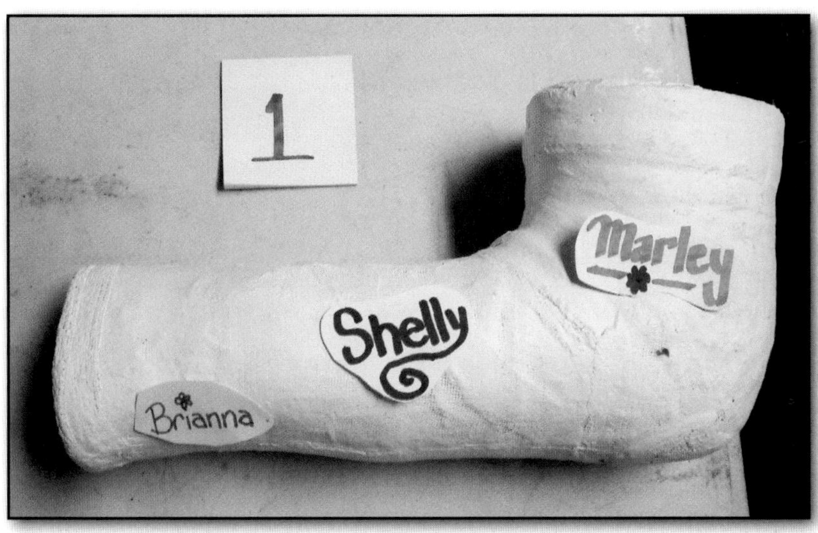

The end result was an amazingly realistic series of casts. And Robert reports that they were itchy, just like the real thing.

The propmaster was also in charge of creating a lot of the food you see in the movie. He made everything from the fancy cake to the burning casserole Greg pulls out of the oven in the Home Ec scene.

He also made the giant ice cream sundae that the grown-up Greg eats in the mansion fantasy scene. It was made out of shortening, corn syrup, icing sugar, and cocoa powder so it wouldn't melt under the lights.

But not all the food you see in the movie is a prop. Have you ever seen a commercial on TV where someone is saying how good such and such food tastes?

When the cameras stop rolling, the actors usually spit out the food they've got in their mouths. That's because the actors have to do lots of takes, and if they actually swallow the food, they'll eventually get sick.

Sometimes during the filming of a food scene in "Diary of a Wimpy Kid," there wasn't a chance to spit out the food. So don't mention mashed potatoes to Zach Gordon if you run into him.

GARAGE BAND

In the book, Rodrick's band, Löded Diper, practices in his room in the basement.

In the film, they practice in the garage. So why the change? Well, in Vancouver, there aren't a whole lot of houses with finished basements. And even if there were, it would be really tough to cram a whole film crew and actors into an underground room. So Löded Diper became a garage band instead.

Only one of the actors who played the Löded Diper bandmates had ever been in a real band, and that was the lead singer.

The actors met just a few minutes before they made their big entrance in the Löded Diper van.

HEY, WE MISSED A SHOT!

At the end of each day, all the raw footage from that day's filming is collected in one place and burned onto DVDs. These DVDs are called "dailies," and they give the director, the producers, and the executives back at the studio a chance to see how the movie's coming along. Dailies also give everyone a chance to see if something's been missed. Sometimes there's not enough "coverage" for a particular scene, which means the director has to shoot additional film to capture the part that's missing.

DIARY OF A WIMPY KID

9/14/09

The problem is, you can't always go back to the place where you shot the scene originally. So you have to fake it. This is what happened with the cafeteria scene.

The filmmakers realized they needed more coverage of the scene where Fregley, Greg, and Rowley are sitting against a cinderblock half-wall. But school was back in session at Templeton, and the film crew couldn't shoot there.

So a fake cinderblock wall was made out of styrofoam and painted to look like the one in the cafeteria. Then a blue screen was put up behind the wall and the scene was reshot.

When you see the boys sitting against the wall in the cafeteria, the actors are really in the Heffleys' garage—in the exact spot where Löded Diper practices.

PAGE TO SCREEN

Here are a few of the Halloween scenes that made their way from the book to the movie.

OOH OOH!
EEE EEE!
AHH AHH!
HOO!
HOO!
AHHHHHHHH...

DO IT IN ONE TAKE

Even though each scene is usually filmed lots of times, there are some you don't really want to film more than once. One of those scenes was when Greg and Rowley get water dumped on their heads by Greg's dad at the end of Halloween night.

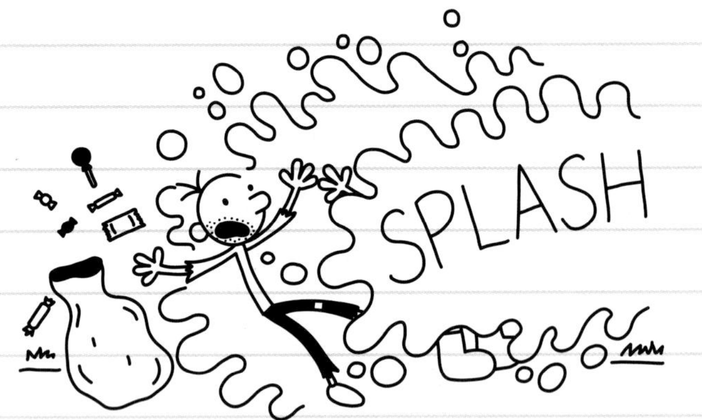

When the scene was filmed, it was October, and it was starting to get chilly in Vancouver. Nobody wanted the actors to get soaked more times than they had to.

Plus, if the shot wasn't perfect, the actors would have to be dried off and given new costumes. So it was important to get it right the first time.

In the movie, Mr. Heffley dumps the water on the kids from a second-story window. But when the shot was filmed, two men stood offscreen, each holding a bucket of water. The men practiced a few throws before the actors took their places.

When the director yelled "Action!" the guys with the buckets tossed the water at Zach and Robert.

They nailed it in one take, and everyone went home happy that night.

ROWLEY JEFFERSON, 007

Some of the actors made good use of their downtime on the set. Robert Capron decided to use his free time to produce several James Bond-inspired movie scripts—with Rowley as the star, of course.

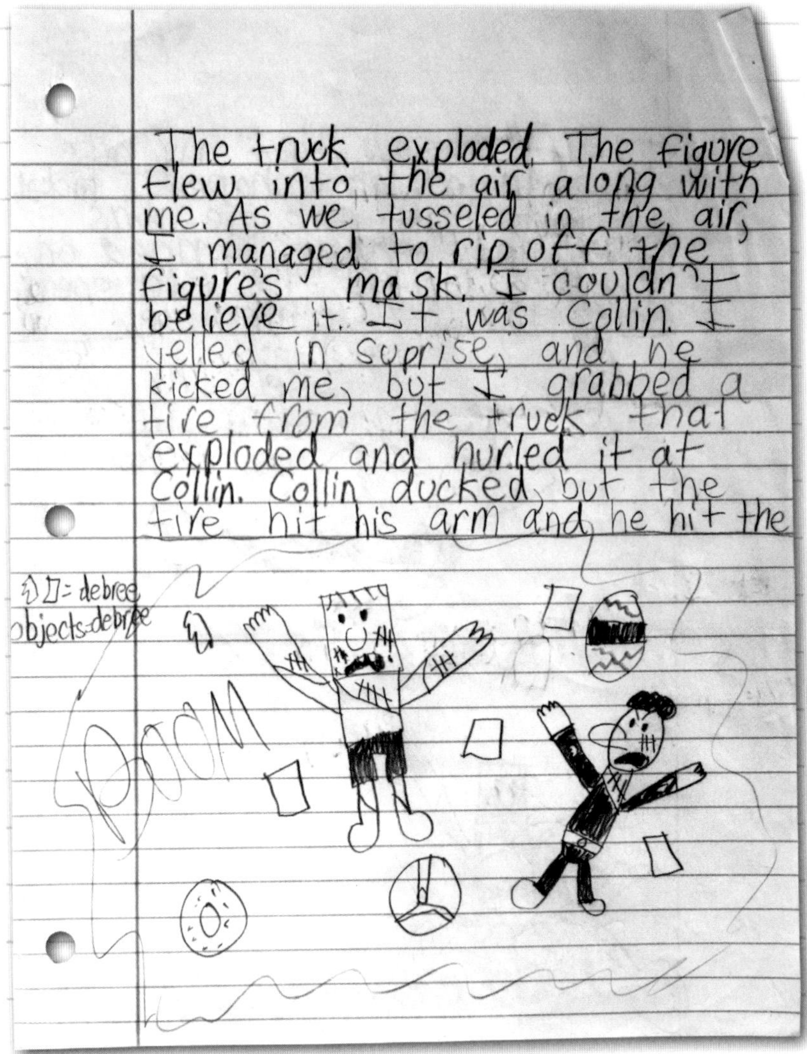

The truck exploded. The figure flew into the air along with me. As we tusseled in the air, I managed to rip off the figure's mask. I couldn't believe it. It was Collin. I yelled in suprise, and he kicked me, but I grabbed a tire from the truck that exploded and hurled it at Collin. Collin ducked, but the tire hit his arm and he hit the

While on the set, Robert worked on "The Friend Who Hated Me," "On Her Principal's Secret Service," and a few others. Here's the big romantic moment in "From Westmore with Love"—

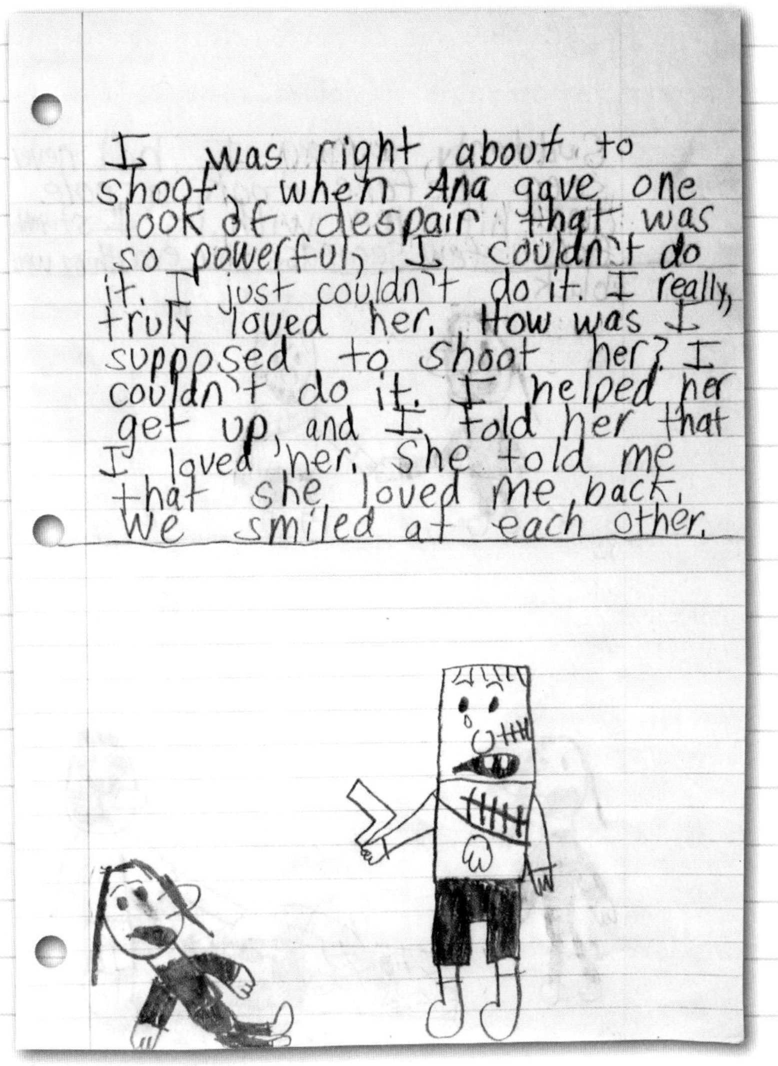

I was right about to shoot, when Ana gave one look of despair that was so powerful, I couldn't do it. I just couldn't do it. I really, truly loved her. How was I supposed to shoot her? I couldn't do it. I helped her get up, and I told her that I loved her. She told me that she loved me back. We smiled at each other.

MOVING IT INDOORS

October in Vancouver means rain, so after the Halloween scenes were filmed, it was time to move things indoors.

The whole operation was relocated to a soundstage on a movie lot nearby. A soundstage is like a big empty airplane hangar where sets are built for a movie.

So why build sets on a soundstage when you can use real buildings and homes instead? Well, there are a few reasons.

The first is the weather. If you're working on a soundstage, you're in an environment where you don't have to worry about rain, snow, or the cold, because there's a roof over your head.

Another reason is convenience. If you build a few sets in one place, you don't have to keep moving the actors, film crew, and equipment around. That saves time, and you can get more work done.

But the main reason to use a soundstage is to build the kinds of sets you can't find in the real world. Sometimes you need to be able to move cameras around so you can film from lots of different angles, and that's tough to do in a small room in a real building. On a soundstage set, you can remove walls to give yourself more space.

The set designers built three rooms on the soundstage: the Heffleys' kitchen, Greg's bedroom, and Rodrick's attic. It might seem strange that these three rooms had to be built, since they existed in the real homes, but since so many scenes were filmed in these spots, it made sense to create them on a soundstage.

Building a set is just like building a real structure. You need carpenters, electricians, and painters. You even need a draftsman to come up with the plans. Here's a blueprint of the Heffleys' kitchen—

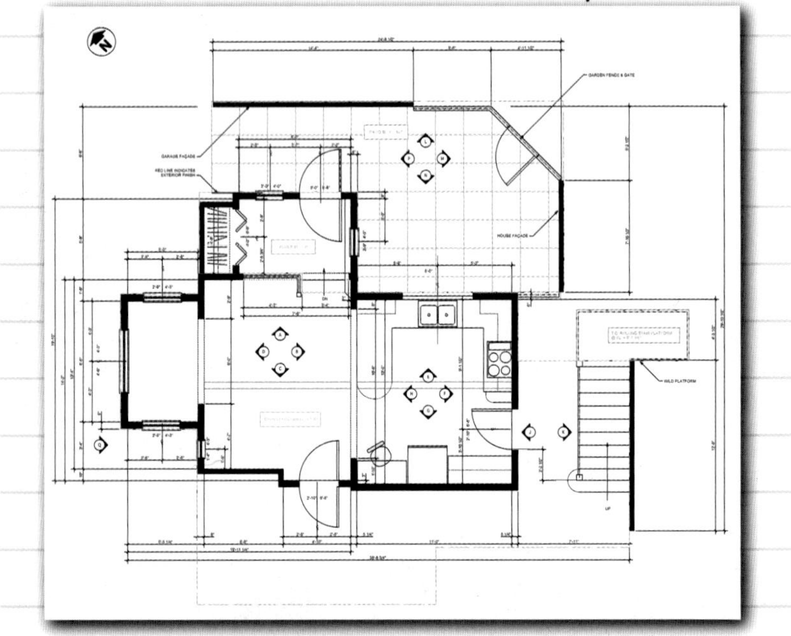

Everything you see on the screen is planned down to the smallest detail. Even the windows had to be designed.

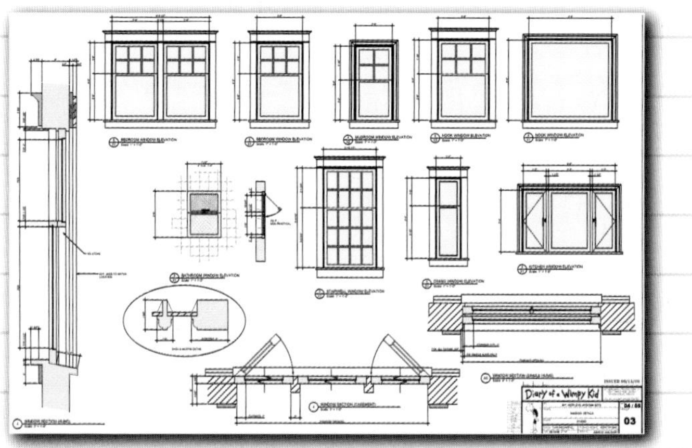

After the set decoration group did their work in the kitchen, it looked like a busy family had been using it for years.

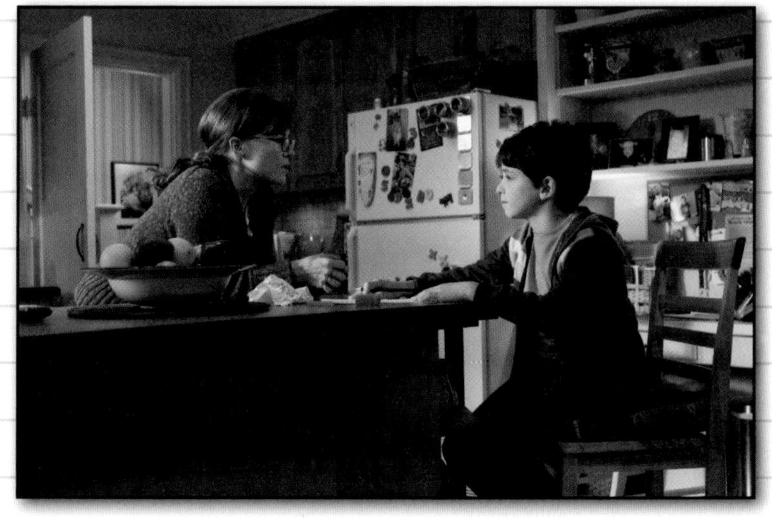

ROOM FOR INTERPRETATION

When it came to designing Greg's bedroom, the art department didn't have a lot to go on. There's just not a lot of information in the book's drawings.

It was up to the set designers and decorators to imagine what Greg's room would look like in the real world.

The first thing they decided was that Greg's room should look authentic—it shouldn't look like a room created for a few scenes in a movie.

The set designers and decorators wanted to make it look like a real kid lived in the room, and had lived there for a long time.

Most kids go through a lot of different interests and hobbies over the years, and their rooms end up being a kind of museum of the things they liked at one time or another. If you look closely at Greg's room, you can see old cowboy toys, a rock collection, monster models, and airplane kits.

The set decorators decided that Greg is currently in a pirate phase, which is why he dresses up as one for Halloween.

The constant shifting in his interests tells you something about Greg. He's got a short attention span and is always moving on to the next thing. In that way, he's very different from Rowley, who seems happy to stay a child forever.

When the set decorators were coming up with the stuff to hang on Greg's walls, they had one serious challenge. Remember, everything in "Diary of a Wimpy Kid" is supposed to look timeless, so the audience shouldn't be able to tell when the story takes place. But most boys have posters of current movies, bands, and sports stars hanging up.

Even though there aren't any sports or band posters in Greg's room, there IS one video game poster hanging on his wall. But of course it's for a game that doesn't exist in real life.

For Rodrick's room, the set designers and decorators had a little more to work with. Here's a picture of Greg going through Rodrick's dresser drawer in the book—

Rodrick's room is the ultimate teenage hangout. It's got lots of posters of classic heavy-metal bands and other stuff Rodrick would like.

Teenagers like their independence, which is why Rodrick lives separately from the rest of the family, in the attic. Rodrick's room was one of the biggest sets built on the soundstage. Here's what it looked like from the outside, along with the plan created to build it—

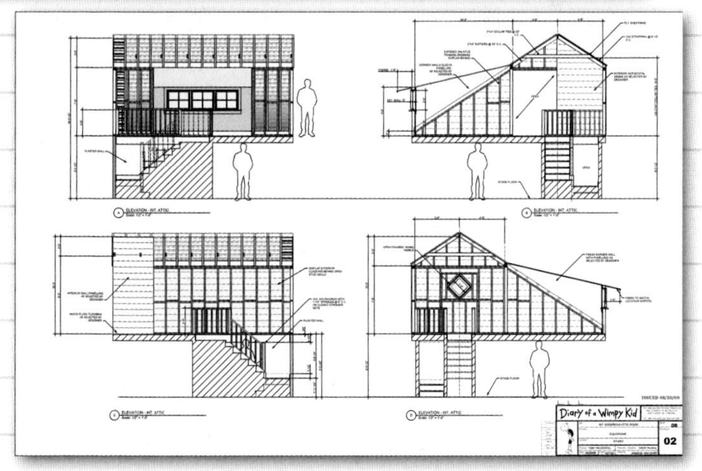

Fregley's bedroom was shot inside a real house, back when the crew was filming on location. But the filmmakers felt there wasn't enough coverage and they needed to get a few more shots of Greg in Fregley's bedroom.

So half of Fregley's bedroom was entirely rebuilt on the soundstage. The set designers and decorators had to place every item in Fregley's room back where it had been in the real room. They used continuity photos from the original room to tell what went where.

When you're watching the movie, see if you can tell which is the soundstage version of Fregley's room and which is the original.

BABY BOYS
FREE GUM
GUM

IT'S A WRAP!

As filming wound down, the actors "wrapped" their final scenes. In one of Robert Capron's last shots, he was dangling from a wire against a blue screen—his close-up reaction to flying through the air during the Big Wheel flip.

Each time an actor wraps, the cast and crew give them a big round of applause and say good-bye.

It isn't always easy for an actor to leave. After working together for a few months, the actors and the crew form a strong bond. So even though actors get to return to their families back home, they're also leaving behind relationships they formed during filming.

Luckily, everyone's invited back at the end of shooting for a big "wrap party," where they can have fun and cut loose.

Ironically, one of Zach Gordon's very last shots was the opening monologue—the scene Zach first performed way back at the beginning, when he tried out for the role of Greg Heffley.

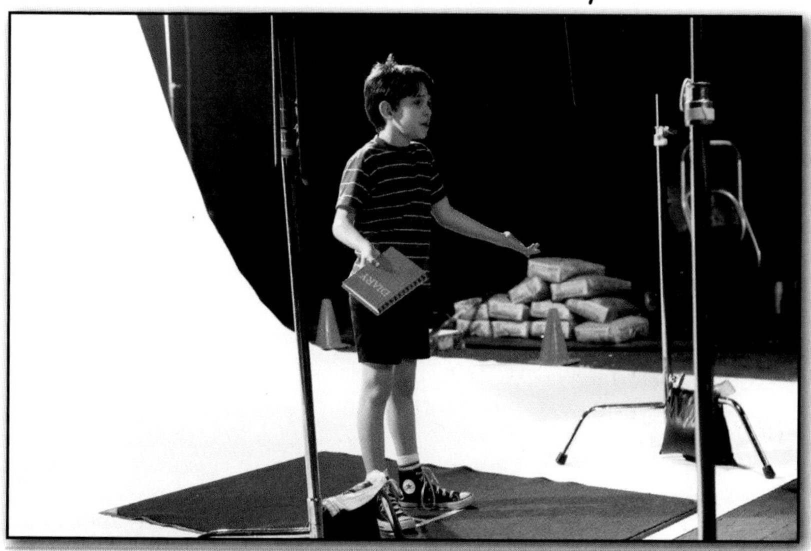

Things had come full circle for Zach. He had spent three months living in Greg Heffley's shoes, and now it was finally time to go home. It was also time for Zach to go to middle school—this time for real.

GREG HEFFLEY, MOVIE STAR

After working on "Diary of a Wimpy Kid" for three months, Zach had gone from being a kid who had done some acting in television shows, commercials, and film to a full-out movie star.

On his last day on the set, a photographer took pictures of Zach for a fantasy sequence in which Greg imagines how life will be once he's famous and his face is on the covers of magazines.

Somehow it seemed like the right way to end things.

PACKING UP

After the actors have gone home, the crew packs up all the sets and props for the movie and puts them in storage. They do this in case certain scenes need to be reshot and in case there's a sequel and some of the sets and items might be used again. Here are a few of the props before they got packed away in boxes—

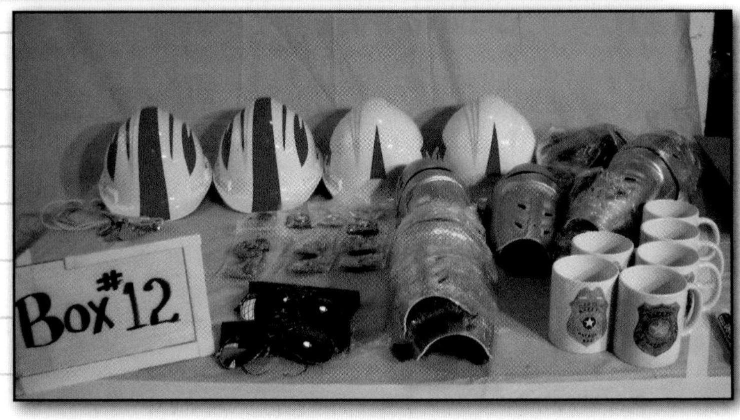

Box #14

BACK BRACE
MOUTH GUARD
WESTMORE
MIDDLE SCHOOL
KNOW NO BOUNDS!
DIARY
Box #VFX

Box #28

PUTTING THE PIECES IN PLACE

After a movie's finished shooting, it's still got a long way to go before it's ready to be seen by an audience. In fact, the work that's done AFTER a movie wraps actually takes longer than filming itself. This phase of the work is called "postproduction," and it includes everything from adding visual and sound effects to creating the closing credits. But the biggest job is editing.

Editing means going through the mountain of footage that's been filmed and picking out the best parts, then combining them into a story. The film editor and the director work closely for several months piecing the movie together.

Editors have one of the most important jobs in the moviemaking process, because they help decide how the story will finally get onto the screen.

When the director films a movie, he creates little shots that are like puzzle pieces—all out of order. The editor chooses the best parts of what the actors have done, sometimes cutting the scenes and even changing the words the actors say.

The editor can rearrange all the pieces to tell the story in different ways. Some people call this the "final rewrite." Another way to think of it is as the "elastic version," because it's the last chance to change the story.

One of the toughest puzzles for the editor to put together was the scene where Greg tosses the kindergartners into the muddy pit.

First of all, the downpour made things tough for Zach and the five-year-old kids, and good clips were hard to find.

When the kindergartners were tossed into the pit by Zach, there was someone in the hole to catch them. Since there was a springy pad in the pit, sometimes the kids would bounce back up into view. The editor had to make sure to find clips where the kids couldn't be seen popping up.

Good sound was also hard to come by, because people were shouting directions and encouragement to the young actors from across the street while the cameras were rolling.

Finally, in the shot where the kids look up at Mrs. Irvine, the kindergartners had to look into the rain, and it was hard for them to keep their eyes open.

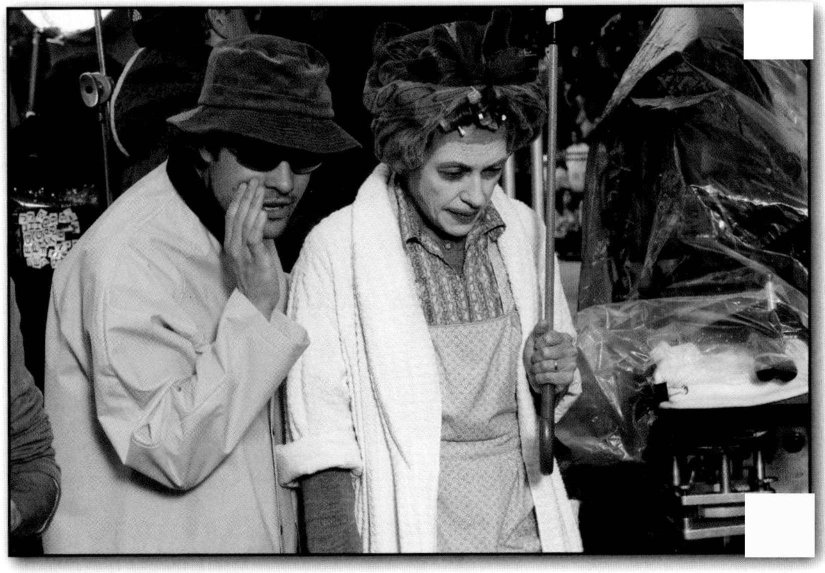

All this made for a challenge for the editor, but she was able to find the right pieces to put the puzzle together.

SOUND DECISIONS

Another big piece of the puzzle is sound. Even though some sound gets recorded during filming (like the dialogue spoken by the actors), there's a lot more that gets added during postproduction. Sound effects are created in a "Foley studio," where there are tons of everyday items that can be used to make just about any sound you can imagine. For example, if someone is getting punched in the movie, a recording engineer might smack a watermelon with a stick to make the right sound.

But not all the sounds created during post-production are noise. There's music, too. While the movie was coming together in the editing room, a composer was creating the "score," or background music, for the film.

You might not really notice the score unless you're listening for it, but music is a big part of the movie. The background music reflects what's going on in a scene, and it helps the audience feel what the characters are feeling.

For example, in a scene of Greg and Rowley walking down the street after a good day at school, there might be bouncy, upbeat music in the background. But in one where the characters are scared, high-pitched violins might play to make you feel tense.

A variety of musical styles and instruments were used to reflect the different moods and characters in the movie.

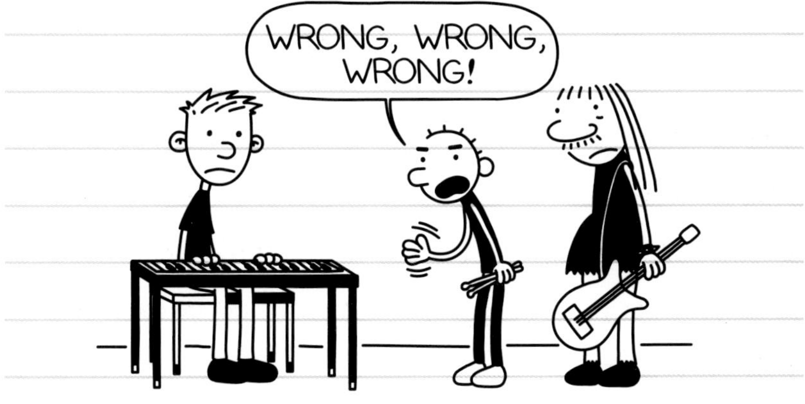

SETTING IT IN MOTION

Most of the "Diary of a Wimpy Kid" movie is live-action, but there are moments when the drawings from Greg's journal come to life on the screen.

It was up to a team of animators to figure out how to make the two-dimensional cartoons in the book look interesting and lively when they moved.

Here's an illustration from the book—

In order to give the movie version of this scene depth, the animators re-created it on a computer and placed the characters in a 3-D environment.

Then they converted everything to a rough pencil look to make the whole scene seem like a middle schooler's drawings come to life.

Here's a still shot of the final result—

Here's how one animated scene came together.

In the movie, Greg imagines himself stuck with Fregley on a deserted island. First, Thor created a storyboard to show the position of the characters. Then a more refined pencil sketch was drawn.

Next, the animators created a "wireframe" version of the drawing, which made the 2-D sketch into a 3-D model that animators could manipulate.

After that, the animators "painted" the wireframe to create the shaded version. This gave them an idea of how the characters looked as solid shapes.

For the finished product, the shading was removed, leaving only the black lines.

TESTING THE WATERS

Before a movie is released, the studio invites a group of people in to watch a "test screening," or preview. The reason for a test screening is to see how an audience reacts to a movie.

Is the audience laughing at the right places? Do they seem bored in certain spots? And do they seem scared at the right times?

Showing the movie to an audience is a big moment for the filmmakers, because up until that point they're just guessing how people might respond.

After the test screening, the audience members are handed questionnaires to fill out.

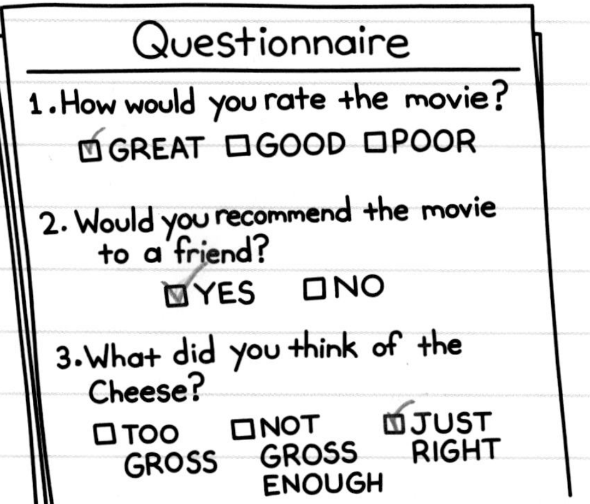
Questionnaire

1. How would you rate the movie?

☑ GREAT ☐ GOOD ☐ POOR

2. Would you recommend the movie to a friend?

☑ YES ☐ NO

3. What did you think of the Cheese?

☐ TOO GROSS ☐ NOT GROSS ENOUGH ☑ JUST RIGHT

The questionnaires help the filmmakers decide if they should change anything in the movie before it's released to the general public. Sometimes what the test screening audience says can have a big impact on the finished film. Other times, not so much.

PUTTING IT OUT THERE

After more than two years of work, it was finally time for the filmmakers to present their film to the world.

Special screenings of the movie gave the actors a chance to reunite with one another for the first time in almost six months. And everyone got a chance to celebrate the work they did together.

Long before "Diary of a Wimpy Kid" hit theaters, Karan Brar, who plays Chirag, drew his vision of what the premiere would look like.

He even predicted a Best Director win for Thor at the Oscars. And who knows?

Of course, all the people involved with the film hope there will be more movies so they'll get to work together again.

But whatever the future holds, everyone who worked on "Diary of a Wimpy Kid" realizes they got to be a part of something special, and the actors will always have a connection to the characters they played.

That goes especially for Zach Gordon, who wasn't afraid to dream big and bring a wimpy kid to life.

SCRAPBOOK

HORNETS

Alpha-Bits

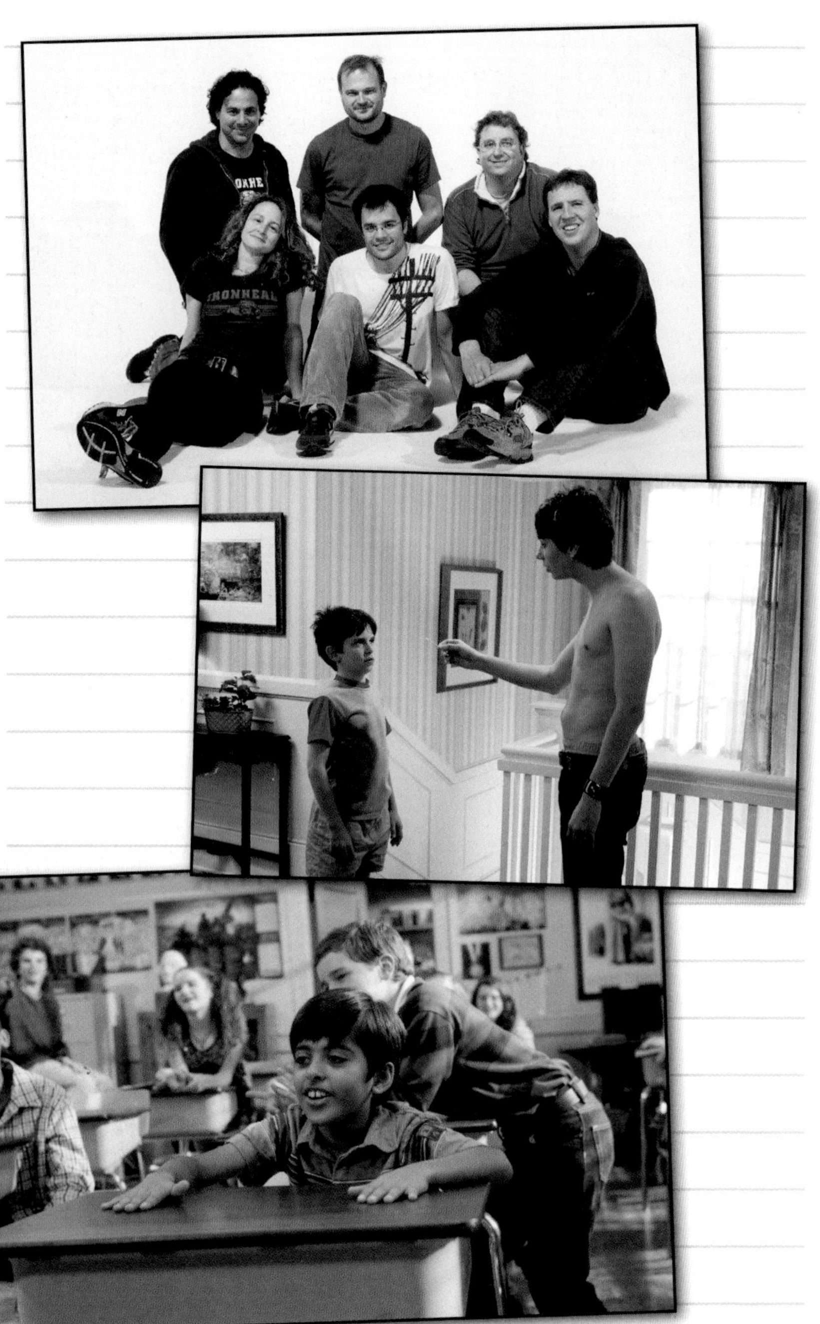

Me & My Mommy
HOME
BALL
STRIKE

CREDITS

FOX 2000 PICTURES Presents

A COLOR FORCE Production

"DIARY OF A WIMPY KID"

Greg Heffley
ZACHARY GORDON

Rowley Jefferson
ROBERT CAPRON

Susan Heffley
RACHAEL HARRIS

and

Frank Heffley
STEVE ZAHN

Music Supervisor
JULIA MICHELS

Music by
THEODORE SHAPIRO

Co-Producer
ETHAN SMITH

Film Editor
WENDY GREENE BRICMONT, A.C.E.

Production Designer
BRENT THOMAS

Director of Photography
JACK GREEN, ASC

Executive Producer
JEFF KINNEY

Produced by
NINA JACOBSON
BRAD SIMPSON

Based upon the book by
JEFF KINNEY

Screenplay by
JACKIE FILGO & JEFF FILGO
and GABE SACHS & JEFF JUDAH

Directed by
THOR FREUDENTHAL

FOX 2000 PICTURES PRESENTS A COLOR FORCE PRODUCTION "DIARY OF A WIMPY KID"
ZACHARY GORDON ROBERT CAPRON RACHAEL HARRIS AND STEVE ZAHN MUSIC SUPERVISOR JULIA MICHELS MUSIC BY THEODORE SHAPIRO
CO-PRODUCER ETHAN SMITH FILM EDITOR WENDY GREENE BRICMONT, A.C.E. PRODUCTION DESIGNER BRENT THOMAS DIRECTOR OF PHOTOGRAPHY JACK GREEN, ASC EXECUTIVE PRODUCER JEFF KINNEY
PRODUCED BY NINA JACOBSON BRAD SIMPSON BASED UPON THE BOOK BY JEFF KINNEY SCREENPLAY BY JACKIE FILGO & JEFF FILGO AND GABE SACHS & JEFF JUDAH
DIRECTED BY THOR FREUDENTHAL www.diaryofawimpykidmovie.com Read the *Diary of a Wimpy Kid* series from Amulet Books

DOLBY

20th CENTURY FOX

ACKNOWLEDGMENTS

Just as it took an army of talented people to make the movie, it took contributions from a big cast of characters to make this book. Thanks to everyone at Fox—especially Carla Hacken, Elizabeth Gabler, Riley Ellis, and Nick D'Angelo—for believing in *Diary of a Wimpy Kid* enough to make it into a film. Thanks to producers Nina Jacobson and Brad Simpson for putting your heart and soul into the movie and for shepherding me through the process for the first time. Thanks to Thor Freudenthal for doing a great job directing the movie and for contributing to this book with your storyboards and journal pages. Thanks to Monique Prudhomme for your outstanding costumes and for helping me understand the thinking that goes into your craft. Thanks to Brent Thomas for your insight into the work that goes on in the production department, and to all of the graphic artists, set designers, and set decorators whose work I've displayed in this book. Thanks to Warren Carr for sharing your team's work with me and for offering your help so readily. Thanks to propmaster extraordinaire David Dowling for being so generous with your time and for explaining everything that goes into your work. Thanks to Tony O'Dell for taking the time to share your thoughts on being an acting coach and for being such a great role model to the kids on the set. Thanks to unit photographer Rob McEwan, whose beautiful work is seen throughout this book. Thanks to Jeff and Jackie Filgo for taking on the challenge of transforming the book into a script and for helping me understand the art of screenwriting. Thanks to Gabe Sachs and Jeff Judah for seeing the project to the end and for your terrific contributions to the script. Thanks to Mike Murphy and Mark Dornfeld for your team's dedication to the art of visual effects and for working with me to make the animated *Wimpy* world look like the one in the book. Thanks to stunt coordinator Dave Hospes for describing in great detail the planning and effort your team puts into its work. Thanks to Wendy Greene Bricmont for sharing your insights on editing during a very busy time. Thanks to cinematographer Jack Green for lending your extraordinary talents to this film. Thanks to Ethan Smith for your kindness and help. Thanks to Virginia King and Debbie Olshan for helping navigate uncharted territory to make this unusual book. Thanks to Zach Gordon and Robert Capron for stepping into the shoes of my characters and for knocking it out of the park. Thanks to Linda Gordon for all your contributions to this book and for your great help and insight. Thanks to Robert Capron Sr. for taking time to make sure I got everything right. Thanks to Karan Brar for sharing your talents and enthusiasm. Thanks to Jane Fielding for the terrific pictures of your sons. Thanks to all the great folks at Abrams for pulling off the impossible and getting this book out on time, especially Chad W. Beckerman, Veronica Wasserman, and Scott Auerbach. Thanks to my agent, Sylvie Rabineau, for being a guiding force and a great friend. Thanks to my lawyers, Ike Williams, Paul Sennott, and Keith Fleer, for pulling this one off. Thanks to Julie, Will, and Grant for giving up so much of your time with me so I could write this book. And thanks especially to Charlie Kochman, who sat side by side with me to make this happen.

KICK
B
2
A
RRIPPP
Greg